AVRO LANCASTER

GREAT AIRCRAFT OF WORLD WAR II
AVRO LANCASTER
AN ILLUSTRATED GUIDE SHOWN IN OVER 100 IMAGES

MIKE SPICK

LORENZ BOOKS

This edition is published by Lorenz Books,
an imprint of Anness Publishing Ltd,
108 Great Russell Street,
London WC1B 3NA;
info@anness.com

www.lorenzbooks.com; www.annesspublishing.com

Anness Publishing has a new picture agency outlet for images for publishing, promotions
or advertising. Please visit our website www.practicalpictures.com for more information.

Publisher: Joanna Lorenz
Senior Editor: Felicity Forster
Production Controller: Pirong Wang

PUBLISHER'S NOTE
Although the advice and information in this book are believed to be accurate
and true at the time of going to press, neither the authors nor the publisher can
accept any legal responsibility or liability for any errors or omissions that may have
been made nor for any inaccuracies nor for any loss, harm or injury that
comes about from following instructions or advice in this book.

Page 1: **Gibson leads his crew aboard Lancaster ED932, AJ-G, prior to taking off on the Dams Raid.**
Page 2: **Fitters swarm all over the port inner engine of this Lancaster Mk II of No. 408 'Goose' Squadron, RCAF.**
Page 3: **Some Lancaster squadrons removed their dorsal turrets to improve performance.**
Below: **Ice cream cornets among the bombs denoting raids on *Dante's Daughter* of No. 103 Squadron.**

CONTENTS

INTRODUCTION

Bielefeld, western Germany, 14 March 1945. The Lancaster B.l (Special) heading towards its target had been unable to reach more than 14,000ft (4,250m). Beneath it bulked the outline of the largest and most destructive bomb ever used in war – the Grand Slam, weighing more than 22,000lb (10 tonnes). In the nose lay the bomb-aimer, holding the graticule of his sight on the target. The seconds ticked away interminably until at last the computer automatically released the huge bomb.

The pilot, Squadron Leader Calder, felt the bomber lift as the weight came off, and the wings, which previously had taken on a distinct upward curve, resumed their normal shape.

Lying prone in the nose, the bomb aimer watched as the huge weapon plunged downwards, dwindling in size as it did so, spinning as it went for greater accuracy. At first it appeared that it was going to fall short, but this was illusory. In the final seconds of its fall it seemed to sweep forward and hit about 90ft (30m) from the target.

■ TARGET COLLAPSED ■

The impact was not very spectacular; from that altitude there was just a tiny splash of mud as the Grand Slam, travelling faster than sound, penetrated something like 75ft (25m) into the earth. After an 11-second delay, however, a gigantic underground explosion erupted, flinging earth and mud some 500ft (150m) into the air, and forming an enormous cavity into which a large section of the target, a rail viaduct that was vital to German communications during the closing months of the war, collapsed.

Above: The Bielefeld Rail Viaduct had survived previous raids, but succumbed to the first Grand Slam dropped.

The Lancaster had not been flying alone – that would have been far too risky, even at this late stage in the war. It was accompanied by 14 others, each armed with a Tallboy, a smaller (12,000lb/5.4 tonnes) version of the Grand Slam. Even as the huge bomb went off, Tallboys were falling around the viaduct, their combined effect destroying several more arches of the now sadly battered target, and ensuring that it would never again be used to carry German reinforcements to where they were most needed.

The Lancaster had, in the space of three short years, become the backbone of RAF Bomber Command. A total of 7,366 were built, of which almost half were lost on operations. They carried out something like 156,000 operational sorties, an average of about 21 sorties each, which says much about the hazards they faced, and dropped more than 600,000 tons of bombs; an average of more than 81 tons each. They carried greater bomb loads farther than any other wartime bomber.

■ VERSATILITY ■

Lancasters formed the main equipment of the Pathfinder Force – they pioneered low-level marking and precision attacks, and, far more than any other heavy bomber type before or since, they proved amenable to modification to carry special weapons. With all this, the Lancaster retained its docile handling, even when badly damaged, which undoubtedly saved the lives to many crewmen. Long after the war, the Lancaster retains a mystique unequalled by any other bomber, and the affection of those that flew to war in it remains even today.

Above: Grand Slam, the largest bomb of all. Only 41 were dropped, all by Lancaster Specials of No. 617 Squadron.

Above: 1,000lb (450kg) bombs in storage. Lancasters dropped no fewer than 217,640 of these betwen 1942 and 1945.

AVRO LANCASTER MK III

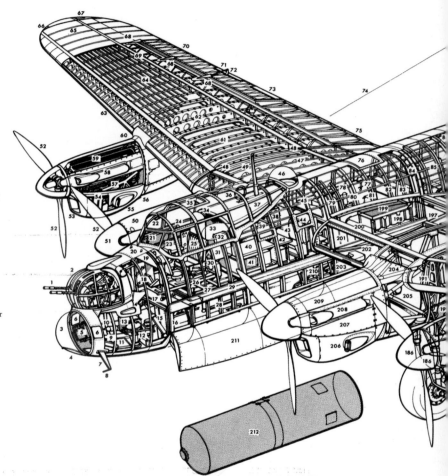

1   Two .303in (7.7mm) Browning machine-guns
2   Frazer-Nash power-operated nose turret
3   Nose blister
4   Bomb-aimer's panel (optically flat)
5   Bomb-aimer's control panel
6   Side windows
7   External air temperature thermometer
8   Pitot head
9   Bomb-aimer's chest support
10 Fire extinguisher
11 Parachute emergency exit
12 F-24 camera
13 Glycol tank/step
14 Ventilator fairing
15 Bomb-bay doors forward actuating jacks
16 Bomb-bay doors forward actuating jacks
17 Control linkage
18 Rudder panels
19 Instrument panel
20 Windscreen sprays
21 Windscreen
22 Dimmer switches
23 Flight-engineer's folding seat
24 Flight-engineer's control panel
25 Pilot's seat
26 Flight-deck floor level
27 Elevator and rudder control rods (underfloor)
28 Trim tab control cables
29 Main floor/bomb-bay support longeron
30 Fire extinguisher
31 Wireless installation
32 Navigator's seat
33 Canopy rear/down-view blister
34 Pilot's head armour
35 Cockpit canopy emergency escape hatch
36 D/F loop
37 Aerial mast support
38 Electrical services panel
39 Navigator's compartment window
40 Navigator's desk
41 Aircraft and radio compass receiver
42 Wireless-operator's desk
43 Wireless-operator's seat
44 Wireless-operator's compartment window
45 Front spar carry-through/ fuselage frame
46 Astrodome
47 Inboard section wing ribs
48 Spar join
49 Aerial mast
50 Starboard inboard engine nacelle
51 Spinner
52 Three-blade de Havilland constant-speed propellers
53 Oil cooler intake
54 Oil cooler radiator
55 Carburettor air intake
56 Radiator shutter

57 Engine bearer frame
58 Exhaust flame-damper shroud
59 Packard-built Rolls-Royce Merlin 28 liquid-cooled engine
60 Nacelle/wing fairing
61 Fuel tank bearer ribs
62 Intermediate ribs
63 Leading-edge structure
64 Wing stringers
65 Wingtip skinning
66 Starboard navigation light
67 Starboard formation light
68 Aileron hinge fairings
69 Wing rear spar
70 Starboard aileron

71 Aileron balance tab
72 Balance tab control rod
73 Aileron trim tab
74 HF aerial
75 Split trailing-edge flap (outboard section)
76 Emergency (ditching) exit
77 Crash axe stowage
78 Fire extinguisher
79 Hydraulic reservoir
80 Signal/flare pistol stowage
81 Parachute stowage box/spar step
82 Rear spar carry-through
83 Bunk backrest
84 Rear spar fuselage frame

85 Emergency packs
86 Roof light
87 Dinghy manual release cable (dinghy stowage in starboard wingroot)
88 Mid-gunner's parachute stowage
89 Tail turret ammunition box
90 Ammunition feed track
91 Emergency (ditching) exit
92 Flame floats stowage
93 Sea markers stowage
94 Roof light
95 Dorsal turret fairing
96 Frazer-Nash power-operated dorsal turret

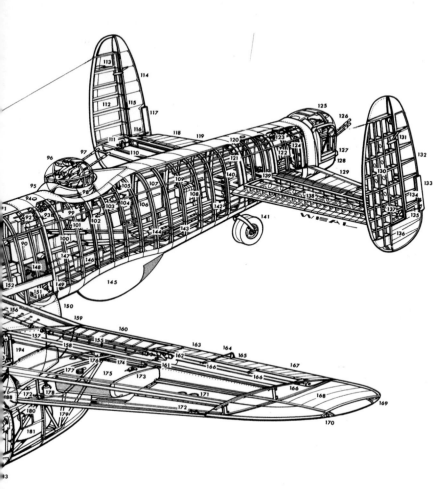

157 Flap tube connecting link
158 Rear spar
159 Split trailing-edge flap
    (inboard section)
160 Split trailing-edge flap
    (outboard section)
161 Aileron control lever
162 Aileron trim tab control
    cable linkage
163 Aileron trim tab
164 Aileron balance tab control rod
165 Aileron balance tab
166 Aileron hinge fairings
167 Port aileron
168 Port wingtip
169 Port formation light
170 Port navigation light
171 Retractable landing lights
    (port wing only)
172 Cable cutters
173 Fuel vent pipe
174 Aileron control rod
175 Port outer (No. 3) fuel tank
    (114 gal/518 litres)
176 Outboard engine support
    frame/rear spar pick-up
177 Fuel booster pump
178 Fire extinguisher
179 Engine sub-frame
180 Filler cap
181 Outboard engine oil tank
182 Firewall/bulkhead
183 Carburettor air intake
184 Outboard engine support frame
185 Port mainwheel
186 Undercarriage oleo struts
187 Flame-damper shroud
188 Outboard engine support
    frame/main spar pick-up
189 Undercarriage retraction jacks
190 Oleo strut attachment pin
191 Undercarriage support beam
    (light-alloy casting)
192 Centre-section outer
    rib/undercarriage support
193 Location of port intermediate
    (No. 2) fuel tank (383 gal/
    1,741 litres)
194 Mainwheel well
195 Emergency retraction air valve
196 Retraction cylinder attachment
197 Port inner (No. 1) fuel tank
    (580 gal/2,637 litres)
198 Oxygen bottle stowage
199 Rest bunk
200 Main spar
201 Hinged inboard leading-edge
202 Cabin heater installation
203 Air intake
204 Inboard engine support frame
205 Inboard engine oil tank
206 Carburettor intake
    anti-ice guard
207 Port inner nacelle
208 Flame-damper shroud
209 Detachable cowling panels
210 Bomb shackles
211 Bomb-bay doors (open)
212 8,000lb (2,532kg) bomb

97 Two .303in (7.7mm) Browning
   machine-guns
98 Turret mounting ring
99 Turret mechanism
100 Ammunition track cover plate
101 Turret step bracket
102 Header tank
103 Oxygen cylinder
104 Fire extinguisher
105 DR compass housing
106 Handrail
107 Crew entry door (starboard)
108 Parachute stowage
109 First-aid pack
110 Starboard tailplane
111 Rudder control lever
112 Starboard tailfin
113 Rudder balance weights
114 Starboard rudder
115 Rudder datum hinge
116 Rudder tab actuating rod
117 Rudder tab

118 Starboard elevator
119 Elevator balance tab
120 Roof light
121 Tail main frame
122 Parachute stowage
123 Fire extinguisher
124 Tail turret entry door
125 Frazer-Nash power-operated
    tail turret
126 Four .303in (7.7mm) Browning
    machine-guns
127 Cartridge case ejection chutes
128 Rear navigation light
129 Elevator trim tab
130 Fin construction
131 Rudder balance weights
132 Port rudder frame
133 Rudder trim tab
134 Rudder tab balance weight
135 Rudder tab actuating rod
136 Rudder horn balance
137 Trim tab actuating jack

138 Tailplane construction
139 Elevator torque tube
140 Tailplane carry-through
141 Non-retractable tailwheel
142 Elsan closet
143 Ammunition track cover plate
144 Elevator and rudder
    control rods
145 H2S (radar-bombing) ventral
    antenna fairing
146 Dorsal turret step
147 Ammunition feed track
148 Tail turret ammunition box
149 Bomb-bay aft bulkhead
150 Bomb-bay doors
151 Bomb-bay doors aft
    actuating jacks
152 Reserve ammunition boxes
153 Main floor support structure
154 Flap operating hydraulic jack
155 Flap operating tube
156 Flap toggle links

THE LANCASTER DESCRIBED

It has often been said that the Lancaster arose from the failure of the Manchester. This is not entirely true – as early as the autumn of 1938, long before the first flight of the Manchester prototype, A.V. Roe's design office considered the possibility of a four-engined variant of the Type 679. But with other priorities in the design offices, only the most basic work was done at this stage on what was to become the Avro Type 683.

Early in the following year, a new specification was issued: B.l/39. Its ultimate purpose was to produce a heavy bomber which would start to replace the four-engined Stirlings and Halifaxes (neither of which had yet flown), and the Manchester itself in four to five years' time.

The requirements were stringent: a cruising speed of 280mph (450km/hr) at 15,000ft (4,570m) while carrying a bomb load of 9,000lb (4.08 tonnes), only slightly less than the maximum of 10,000lb (4.54 tonnes) specified. Range under these conditions was to be a

Left: As a safeguard against a shortage of Merlins, the Mk II Lancaster was powered by Bristol Hercules radial engines. Only 300 were built.

minimum of 2,500 miles (4,000km). This was pushing the state of the art very hard, and was not helped by the requirement for defensive armament, which was to consist of tail and ventral turrets each carrying four 20mm cannon. These turrets did not even exist at that time, and the complexity, weight and drag of such monsters eventually ensured that they never would. Prototype aircraft were ordered from both Handley Page and Bristol, but neither got past the mockup stage. The Air Ministry was however interested in A.V. Roe's proposal for a four-engined bomber developed from the Manchester, even though it would retain the same defensive armament as the latter. But with war looming, the twin-engined aircraft naturally had first priority, and initial

Above: The first four-engined bomber to enter service with Bomber Command was the Short Stirling. It was inferior to the Lancaster in both performance and load-carrying.

progress with the four-engined machine was slow. Not until the production Manchester was finalized could serious work start on its derivative.

With hindsight, the advantages of four-engined bombers seem glaringly obvious. Because they were bigger than their twin-engined counterparts, they could carry heavier loads of fuel and weaponry, which translated into larger bomb loads carried further. In 1939 this was less obvious, and in fact the twin-engined Manchester could carry a 40 per cent greater bomb load than the

BRITISH BOMBER COMPARISONS 1941

Aircraft type	Cruise speed at altitude	Bomb load for maximum radius	Radius with maximum bomb load
Wellington	170mph (273km/hr) at 11,300ft (3,450m)	2,500lb (1,130kg) for 1,100 miles (1,770km)	560 miles (900km) with 4,500lb (2,040kg)
Stirling	208mph (335km/hr) at 13,800ft (4,200m)	3,500lb (1,590kg) for 855 miles (1,375km)	285 miles (460km) with 14,000lb (6,350kg)
Halifax	203mph (327km/hr) at 15,100ft (4,600m)	5,800lb (2,630kg) for 910 miles (1,465km)	580 miles (930km) with 8,000lb (3,630kg)
Manchester	205mph (330km/hr) at 13,650ft (4,160m)	8,100lb (3,675kg) for 885 miles (1,425km)	500 miles (805km) with 10,350lb (4,700kg)

From this table it can be seen that the payload/range of the twin-engined Manchester was significantly better than either of its four-engined contemporaries, whether judged by maximum radius or maximum bomb load. It totally outclassed the earlier twin-engined Wellington in both departments.

Above: The Rolls-Royce Merlin XX engine installation package for the Beaufighter IIF was adapted for the Lancaster.

four-engined Halifax over a comparable distance, although, it must of course be said, this was provided that its Vultures kept running. There were other factors, although these were often rather problematical. Two engines required fewer systems, less installation weight, less maintenance, and lower costs for spares and replacements than four engines. Aerodynamically, with only two engines instead of four, there was the further advantage of having less drag to overcome in flight. The difficult bit was producing an engine that gave sufficient power to do the job, without it becoming too complex to be reliable. Rolls-Royce

was far from the only company to have problems with over-complex engines at this time. The Napier Sabre was scheduled to power the Manchester II, but delays in development ensured this aircraft variant was never built.

The overall wingspan was increased to accommodate engines

The Merlin was the obvious choice for the Type 683, but demand for this engine for Spitfires and Hurricanes, to say nothing of the Whitley and Halifax bombers, was high. As a backup, the

more powerful but heavier and draggier Bristol Hercules radial was selected. Ironically, increased demand for the Hercules caused by Stirling production eventually led to the Beaufighter, originally powered by the Bristol engine, being fitted with Merlin XXs, in its Mk IIF variant. For this, Rolls-Royce had developed an engine installation package, or power egg, which, with minor changes, proved eminently suitable for the new bomber.

Type 683, known in the design office as the Lancaster from a very early stage, was developed around the Manchester fuselage and wing centre section. The crew cabin had been highly praised, while the cavernous bomb bay met all current and not a few future requirements. The overall wingspan was substantially increased to accommodate the outboard engines, which also had the effect of improving take-off performance, while various other detail modifications were made.

■ FOUR ENGINES ■
A turning point came at the end of August 1940, when the decision was taken that Bomber Command's strategic force would be entirely equipped as soon

Left: The Avro Type 683 prototype was initially known as the Manchester III, and only later renamed the Lancaster I.

Above: The second Lancaster prototype introduced a ventral turret that was fitted to early production aircraft.

as possible with four-engined bombers. In retrospect this decision seems extraordinary, if only because the Stirling had barely started reaching its first squadron, while the service entry of the Halifax was still three months in the future, as was that of the Manchester. The four-engined heavy bomber had yet to prove itself, but there remained one sound operational reason for the decision. Even reliable engines failed occasionally, and all were vulnerable to flak and fighters. The failure of one engine in a four-engined type was much less serious than the same case in a twin, in which a full 50 per cent of the available power was lost, and asymmetric handling problems, with all the remaining power on one side, were far more extreme.

Trials at Boscombe Down showed good handling qualities but directional stability was lacking

The decision to proceed with the four-engined Avro bomber was taken, although as a security measure the name Lancaster was dropped and the Type 683 became known as the Manchester Mark III, the Mark II designation having been reserved for the Napier Sabre-

powered aircraft, which in fact was never built. The prototype used a Manchester I air-frame powered by Merlin Xs, and retained the short-span tailplane and triple fin layout of that aircraft. The first flight took place on 9 January 1941.

Trials at Boscombe Down showed good handling qualities although, as was only to be expected, directional stability was lacking This was cured by a new tailplane of almost double the span of the original, and very much larger twin fins and rudders, with the central fin removed. With the new Merlin XXs fitted, the prototype reached a maximum speed of 310mph (500km/hr) at 21,000ft (6,400m) – an outstanding performance for a heavy bomber of that era. A new production contract was issued, limiting the output of Manchesters to 200 before switching to the Lancaster, as it had inevitably become known. The use of Manchester sub-assemblies speeded up this process.

■ SECOND PROTOTYPE ■

The second Lancaster prototype, which made its maiden flight on 13 May 1941, was rather nearer to the production machine standard, stressed for an all-up weight of 60,000lb (27.22 tonnes), and

---

LANCASTER

Dimensions
Wingspan 102ft (31.09m); Length (tail up) 69ft 6in (21.18m); Height (tail up) 20ft 6in (6.25m); Wing area 1,297sq ft (120.45m²).

Weights
Empty 36,900lb (16,740kg); Normal loaded 53,000lb (24,040kg); Maximum overload 65,000lb (29,480kg) (B.I Special with 22,000lb (9,980kg) Grand Slam 70,000lb (31,750kg); Maximum internal bomb load 14,000lb (6,350kg).

Power
Four Rolls-Royce Merlin 12-cylinder liquid-cooled engines each rated at 1,460hp (variable depending on type) driving a three-bladed variable-pitch, constant-speed propeller. Lancaster B.III powered by four Bristol Hercules 14-cylinder air-cooled radial engines each rated at 1,650hp.

Fuel and oil
Total fuel 2,154 gal (9,790 litres) in six wing tanks. 580 gal (2,637 litres) in each inboard wing tank; 383 gal (740 litres) in each intermediate wing tank, and 114 gal (518 litres) in each outboard wing tank. One or two overload 400 gal (1,818 litre) tanks could be mounted in the bomb bay. Oil tank capacity 150 gal (682 litres) carried in four wing tanks.

Performance
Maximum speed 270mph (434km/hr) at 19,000ft (5,800m); Cruise speed 210mph (338km/hr); 19.3 min to 11,000ft (3,350m); 43.5 min to 20,000ft (6,100m); Service ceiling 21,500ft (6,550m); Range with 14,000lb (6,350kg) bomb load 1,160 miles (1,870km); with 7,000lb (1,795kg) bomb load and one overload fuel tank 2,230 miles (3,590km).

Armament
Two .303 Browning machine-guns with 1,000rpg in a Frazer-Nash power-operated turret in the nose; ditto in the mid-upper position, and four Browning machine-guns with 2,500rpg in a Frazer-Nash power-operated turret in the tail. A few aircraft retained the ventral gun position, while many others had the mid-upper turret removed. Others were fitted with a Rose Rice tail turret with two .50 Browning heavy machine-guns.

with a dorsal gun turret fitted. It retained the ventral turret for the time being. This was followed into the air by the third prototype on 26 November of that year, which was powered by Hercules VI radials, and as such became the prototype Lancaster Mark II. But long before the radial-engined machine took to the air, production Mark Is were rolling off the lines.

The production aircraft still showed their Manchester origins, but had been refined in many ways. All-up weight had been increased to 65,000lb (29.48 tonnes) maximum, although this could be exceeded in an emergency; maximum bomb load had been increased to 14,000lb (6.35 tonnes); two extra fuel tanks had been fitted in the wings, and the ventral turret had been deleted as being of no earthly use at night. A collar fairing had been added around the mid-upper turret to prevent the guns being depressed enough to damage the aircraft, and a four-gun turret was standard in the tail position. The crew consisted of seven men: the pilot, who was also the aircraft captain, regardless of rank; a second pilot, who was quickly replaced by the new category of flight engineer; a bomb-aimer, who also manned the front turret; a navigator; a wireless operator; and mid-upper and tail gunners.

■ THE LANCASTER ■ CLOSE UP

The Lancaster is a lady, and for that reason is never described as 'it', but always as 'she'. No empty-headed glamour queen this, frivolous and shallow, but very much the

Above: The standard camouflage scheme was dark green and dark earth disruptive pattern above, and matt black below.

grand dame, the indomitable dowager, yet with a twinkle in her eye to hint at a racy past in her younger days. Her attire is sombre, a staid dull black on undersides of wings and tail and fuselage sides complemented by a tasteful camouflage scheme on top. Guns protrude from turrets in her nose and tail and mid-way down her upper fuselage, saying, as they said to many a German night fighter during the war 'Do not trifle with me, young man!' There she sits on the ground, nose high, seemingly sniffing at the sky, eager to take once more to the element for which she was designed.

As we walk towards her, the first impression is that she is big. Her huge main wheels, suspended on sturdy legs beneath the inboard engine nacelles, are almost shoulder-height, while the front fuselage towers high above us. Her mid-mounted wings spread 50ft (15m) to either side, carrying the four sleek cowlings which house the Rolls-Royce Merlin engines with their shrouded exhausts, fronted by large three-bladed propellers.

We draw nearer. Right in the front of her nose is a hemispherical transparent dome, with a round optically flat panel looking downwards. This is where the real business is done; through this the bombs are aimed. Above is a turret from which project the muzzles of two .303

Below: Figures on the ground give scale to the first production Lancaster, seen prior to delivery to Boscombe Down for type testing.

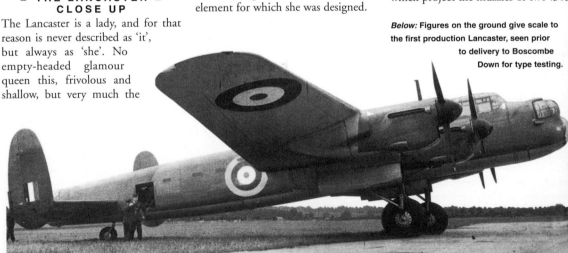

LANCASTER GUN TURRET

Type	FN 5	FN 50	FN 20	FN 64
Position	Nose	Mid-upper	Tail	Ventral*
Guns	2 x .303 Browning Mk II	2 x .303 Browning Mk II	4 x .303 Browning Mk II	2 x .303 Browning Mk II
Rounds per gun	1,000	1,000	2,500	500
Gunsight	Mk III Reflector	Mk IIIA Reflector	Mk III Reflector or Gyro Mk IIe	Periscopic
Traverse	+/-95°	360°	+/-94°	+/-90°
Elevation	60°	20°	60°	0°
Depression	45°	2°	45°	60°

Rarely used, mainly on early aircraft.

Browning machine-guns. Immediately behind the turret is a glazed cabin for the pilot and his flight engineer, but we see little of this as we walk beneath the giant bird.

What we do see is the huge bomb bay, which starts almost immediately beneath the front of the cabin and reaches back beyond the wing trailing edge to a point almost level with the dorsal turret. As is usual before engine start-up, the bomb bay doors are open, revealing the sinister outlines of the contents. In the centre is a large, dark green cylinder, a 4,000lb (1,800kg) high explosive 'cookie'. It is surrounded by twelve SBCs (Small Bomb Containers) filled with incendiaries. This is the most usual Lancaster bomb load.

We climb up and in, then it's down on to the central catwalk

Astern of the bomb bay is a teardrop-shaped fairing. This houses the scanner for H2S , the latest radar bombing and navigational aid. We enter the Lancaster through a small hatch in the starboard side, just ahead of the leading edge of the tailplane. A short metal ladder hooks on to the sill, and we climb up and in, on to an inner step, then it's down on to the central catwalk.

■ REAR GUNNER ■

Once inside, it is difficult to see much until our eyes accustom themselves to the gloom. Not that there is a lot to see; to one accustomed to travel in modern airliners, the interior of a Lancaster is bleak indeed. The structure, fuselage formers and longerons are bare, showing the metal skin. Running the length of the fuselage walls are pipes, rods, all manner of plumbing and wiring. These are for carrying hydraulic fluid and power to where it is needed.

At this point, the first member of the crew leaves us. He turns left and vanishes.

He passes the primitive Elsan toilet to his right, scrambles over the tailplane spar structure, pauses for a moment to stow his parachute, then squeezes into his cold and cramped position, shutting the armoured doors behind him. He is the rear gunner, and his job is arguably the most dangerous, and certainly the coldest, the most lonely and isolated of any Lancaster crewman.

From now until the end of the mission, his only human contact will be the disembodied voices of other crew members over the intercom. His brief is unceasing vigilance for however many hours the mission takes. The German night fighters almost always attack from astern. Yet his task is thankless; if he is lucky enough to survive a complete tour of operations, he may well do so without once so much as seeing a night fighter, but knowing that the one he doesn't see may well kill him and his crew. He is proud of his skills; his party piece is probably putting a pencil in the barrel of one of his guns, then using his power controls to sign his name on a piece of card held up by an obliging ground crewman. But the chances are that he will never get the opportunity to use these skills. Even if he does, his four rifle-calibre machine-guns are far outranged by the cannon of the German night fighters which, if visibility is good enough,

Below: The open doors give some idea of the vast size of the bomb bay. The bombs were released in a preset sequence.

Above: Up the ladder and in. A crew from No. 9 Squadron board their Lancaster ready for a mission.

about in flight. Next to reach his station is the mid-upper gunner. After stowing his parachute in its place high on the right, he climbs into his turret via a step on the left of the fuselage. Access is not easy, however, due to the seat design which forces him to squeeze past it before he can enter.

The mid-upper gunner has only two machine-guns, although his turret can be traversed through 360 degrees, giving him a grandstand view all round. His field of fire is obstructed, however, to the rear by the tailplane and fins, on each side by the wings, engines and propellers, and straight ahead by the navigator's astrodome. The turret is surrounded by a fairing which contains a cam track. By restricting the movement of the guns, this ensures that he cannot damage his own aircraft when firing. When the guns are elevated at 20 degrees or more, turret traverse is fast and smooth, but below this it is much slower. This is to avoid damage to the turret fairing at full

can stand off and shoot at him. Otherwise they can slip in below where, against the dark backdrop of the ground, they are difficult to see, and pull underneath the bomber where his guns cannot reach and pick it off with their upward-firing guns.

Even in defeat, with his aircraft going down in flames or out of control, the rear gunner's fate is a lonely one. The call to bale out is 'Abracadabra Jump, Jump! Abracadabra Jump, Jump!'. It sounds silly, but it has one advantage. It cannot possibly be misunderstood. Nevertheless, it was often not used, and the order given in plain language. On hearing the command to bale out, the rear gunner opens his armoured doors at the rear of his turret, reaches back for his parachute and clips it on to his chest harness. He swivels his turret right round until the open doors are facing outwards, then does a backward roll out into the night sky above a hostile country. This is of course presupposing that his parachute has not been burnt or shot to pieces, that he is still able to turn his turret to the escape position, and that the centrifugal forces exerted by his out-of-control bomber will allow him to make these necessary moves.

The rest of the crew turn to the right along the catwalk. On the far wall is a handrail, very necessary for moving

LANCASTER BOMB LOADS

Bombing, and especially night bombing, was a very imprecise art in the Second World War. Even finding the target was difficult enough; hitting it often seemed next to impossible. The solution adopted was to saturate the target area with bombs – high explosive to demolish buildings, and incendiaries to set the ruins on fire. It was crude, but it was the only practicable means available to Bomber Command. There were, of course, specialized weapons which called for greater accuracy, but these were less common.

AREA BOMBING LOADS

Blast and demolition
1) 1 x 8,000lb (3,630kg) HE plus 6 (max) 500lb (225kg) HE.
2) 14 x 1,000lb (450kg) HE.

Blast, demolition and fire
3) 1 x 4,000lb (1,800kg) HE plus 3 x 1,000lb (450kg) HE plus up to 6 SBCs (Small Bomb Containers) each holding either 236 4lb (2kg) or 24 x 30lb (14kg) incendiaries.
4) 1 x 4,000lb (1,800kg) HE plus up to 12 SBCs. The most common Lancaster load.

Maximum incendiary
5) 14 SBCs.

Deployed tactical targets
6) 1 x 4,000lb (1,800kg) HE plus up to 18,500lb (225kg) HE, some with delayed action fuses.

Low-level attacks
7) 6 x 1,000lb (450kg) HE with delayed action fuses.

Hardened targets, naval installations, ships etc
8) 6 x 2,000lb (900kg) armour piercing with very short delay fuses.

Minelaying
9) Up to six 1,500lb (680kg) or 1,850lb (840kg) mines.

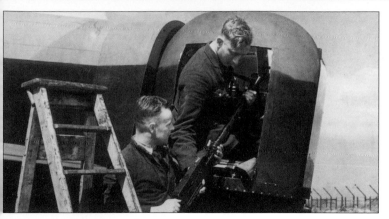

edge of the wing, but at night keeps a curtain drawn across it. This is mainly because he needs artificial light by which to work, and this must not be allowed to betray the presence of the bomber to any roving fighters which might be in the area. In any case, over blacked-out enemy territory there is little to see, while above a heavily defended area the view can sometimes be a little too exciting for someone who has no immediate task to occupy him. The wireless operator has the warmest place in the aircraft; often he is overheated while other crew members are freezing.

Above: Emergency escape from the rear turret was made by turning it sideways, as seen here, then rolling out backwards. *Left:* The mid-upper turret, showing the fairing which prevented the gunner from damaging his own aircraft. *Below:* H2S position in the Lancaster. Top left is the curtain which shuts out light; to the right is the flight engineer's position, with his seat folded. (Alfred Price)

H2S, a blind bombing aid which shows a radar picture of the ground

In front of the wireless operator sits the navigator, sideways on. He also has a table, but larger than that of the wireless operator, on which he spreads out charts, pencils, protractors, computer (not quite like our modern variety), and all the other paraphernalia needed to find a specific location in a blacked-out and hostile Europe. Almost overhead is an astrodome, through which the navigator can 'shoot' the stars to arrive at a very approximate position, but in this machine he has something better and very different.

This is H2S, a blind bombing aid which shows a radar picture of the ground below on a television-type screen. It needs a fair bit of interpretation to get good results, and like all electronic aids of this era, it can be temperamental. But it helps. Like the wireless operator, the navigator has a window, out of which he rarely looks, and he is partitioned off from the pilot by another curtain which keeps light out of the main cabin.

■ THE PILOT ■

Up front, his seat on a raised floor section to the left of the main cabin, is the pilot, who is also the aircraft captain.

depression, but in action it is a serious disadvantage as it makes tracking a fast-moving enemy fighter very difficult.

In an emergency, the mid-upper gunner must squirm out of the turret, retrieve his parachute from stowage, and depart through the door by which he entered. Just ahead of the mid-upper turret is an escape hatch in the fuselage roof, which is used in the event of a crash landing or a ditching at sea. In the latter event, a dinghy is housed in the upper surface of the starboard wingroot, which hopefully can be released manually from inside the aircraft, and which should then inflate automatically if the Lancaster comes down in the 'drink', as it is generally known. The walls in this area of the fuselage are cluttered with fire extinguishers and flame float and sea marker canisters.

Further up the fuselage is an obstacle, the rear wing spar carry-through, with a step on the far side which contains more

parachute stowage. To the left of this is the rest bunk, which is normally used only for casualties.

A few feet along is yet another obstacle, the main wing spar carry-through. Larger than the rear spar, it has probably been the cause of more bad language by Lancaster crewmen than any other feature of this remarkable aircraft, being of a height to make their eyes sparkle. But once this has been negotiated, we arrive at the main crew positions via a 7mm-thick armoured door. Situated on the left is the wireless operator's post. He sits at a small table with his radio and his pencils and pads. He has a small window which is level with the leading

Above: The H2S scanner housing supplanted the ventral turret position on many aircraft. This is a late-war model.
Above right: Lancaster pilot's position, showing the sliding hatch through which escape was barely possible. However, the extensively glazed cabin gave a good all-round view.

He has a good all-round view through the framed canopy, albeit slightly restricted to the rear and to starboard. There is a direct-vision panel on either side of the windshield, and in the canopy roof is an escape hatch, for use in a crash-landing or ditching. Behind him is a 4mm-thick sheet of armour, the top part of which can be folded down.

Straight in front of the pilot is the control column, topped with a wheel-type yoke. The column moves backwards and forwards to control the elevators in the tail, causing the aircraft to climb or dive, while the yoke moves like a car steering wheel, controlling the ailerons in the wings to make the aircraft bank to left or right. At his feet are the rudder pedals, which are used for flat turns to either side.

Low to the pilot's left is the compass, but to allow him to steer without constantly having to glance inside the cockpit a compass repeater is mounted on the centre strut of the divided windshield. On the dash in front of him are many dials and switches, which include the essential flying instruments – air speed indicator, artificial horizon, turn

and bank indicator and rate of climb/descent indicator among them – while the throttle levers and propeller speed controls are mounted on a central console where they can be reached by both the pilot and the flight engineer.

The flight engineer sits to the right of the pilot. He has a folding seat, which is necessary to allow access to the bomb aimer's and front gunner's positions, and a tubular footrest which pulls out from under the raised floor section beneath the pilot's position. His task is to look after the engines, throttle settings and propeller pitch settings, fuel flow, and generally act as the pilot's assistant.

He has two panels to monitor. The first is on the starboard side, and this contains oil and fuel gauges, booster pump switches, fuel pressure warning lights, fuel tank selector cocks, and many other things. The second is part of the main dash, which can also be seen by the pilot. This contains revolution counters, boost gauges, ignition switches, engine fire extinguisher buttons and propeller feathering buttons, plus much else. All in all, the flight engineer is a pretty busy man.

■ BOMB AIMER ■
Squeezing past the flight engineer's station, we clamber down into the nose. Down, because this is the first time that we have been ahead of the bomb bay, and the amount we clamber down gives us some idea of its depth. This is the territory of the bomb aimer, who usually

mans the nose turret when not actually on the bombing run, although he can also be called upon to assist the navigator by map-reading, always assuming that the ground is in sight.

The bomb aimer lies prone, his chest propped on an adjustable support. Beneath him is the forward escape hatch, which may also be used by the flight engineer and the pilot, in the latter case if he can reach it in time before the aircraft goes completely out of control.

To the right of the bomb aimer is the bomb fusing and selection panel. It is essential that the bombs are released in a predetermined order from the long bay if unwanted changes of trim are to be avoided. For this, a selector box is used. The bombs themselves are released by a hand-held 'tit', which has a small guard above the button to prevent accidents. Also featured are camera controls and photo-flares, which enable a picture to be taken of the aim point.

■ BOMBS GONE ■
The bomb sight itself is of the vector type, into which the aircraft speed and altitude are set, together with the ballistic data for the type of bombs carried, and the estimated wind speed and direction. The sight is gyro-stabilized, which allows banked turns to be made during the run-up to the target. Two lines of light on a reflecting screen form a cross which indicates where the bomb will drop at any given moment. Over the intercom, the bomb aimer guides the pilot to a

Left: Bomb release switch in hand, the bomb aimer lies prone facing his Mk XIV vector sight.
Below left: All late-production Lancasters, regardless of mark, were fitted with an enlarged nose transparency.

position where the extension of the vertical line passes through the aim point. When the bomber is lined up correctly, the aim point appears to slide gradually down the vertical line. Then when the cross touches the target, the bomb aimer presses the button and down go the bombs, bringing destruction to the target below. When not engaged in dropping the bombs, the bomb aimer occupies the nose turret, with its two machine-guns. At night he will probably have little to do; rarely is visibility clear enough to allow the night fighters to attack from head-on. In daylight or at low level, the situation may well be different, and it may even be that the turret must be occupied even on the bombing run. This gives rise to a problem: the gunner has no footrest, and in moments of excitement may well tread on the bomb aimer's head, to say nothing of showering him with hot 'empties' when he fires.

This, then, is the Lancaster, a bomber in which many thousands of men went to war, and for which many thousands of crewmen had affection, and faith that she was the best.

Below: When not actually on the bombing run, the bomb aimer normally manned the front gun turret. This Lancaster was visiting the USA on a goodwill mission in 1942.

INTO SERVICE

The first unit to receive the Lancaster was No. 44 (Rhodesia) Squadron at Waddington. To provide initial experience, the first Lancaster prototype arrived in mid-September 1941, while several Manchester pilots were transferred to the squadron to ease the task of conversion. Not until Christmas Eve did the first three operational aircraft arrive, followed by four more on 28 December.

Above: This former No. 44 Squadron aircraft flew the Atlantic to Canada to serve as a pattern aircraft for Lancaster production there.

Far left: Fitters swarm all over the port inner engine of this Lancaster Mk II of No. 408 'Goose' Squadron, RCAF.

No. 44 Squadron had previously flown Hampdens, but from January 1942, seven Manchester squadrons were progressively re-equipped with the Lancaster. Unusually, three of the seven had not even started to receive the Manchester at this time, but this decision was not as strange as it seems. Brand new Manchesters, with their excellent payload/range capability, were still coming off the production lines, and Lancaster production was not yet in full swing. Also, the similarities of the two aircraft made it relatively easy to convert Manchester crews to the Lancaster; the latter could therefore be introduced into service faster by bringing more Manchesters on stream. The first Lancasters reached No. 97 Squadron in January, and No. 207 Squadron in March 1942.

The first Lancaster operation took place on the night of 3/4 March 1942. Four Lancasters of No. 44 Squadron, led by Squadron Leader John Nettleton, laid mines (an operation codenamed 'Gardening') off the German coast. All returned safely. The first excursion over Germany was made a week later, two aircraft of the same squadron joining a raid on Essen, again without loss. This run of good fortune was not to last; the first Lancaster to be lost in action failed to return from another Gardening sortie on 24/25 March.

■ **THE AUGSBURG RAID** ■

In the Spring of 1942 U-boat production facilities became priority targets, and one of the most important was the MAN works at Augsburg, where their diesel engines were made. Augsburg was not far from Munich, a round trip of some 1,250 miles (2,000km), mostly over enemy territory. The works was little bigger than the average football pitch, which ruled out a night attack. The attack would have to be in daylight.

On the afternoon of 17 April, 12 Lancasters took off for Augsburg. The first wave of six, flying in two Vics of three, was from No. 44 Squadron, led by John Nettleton. Two miles (3km) astern and about 3 miles (5km) to starboard was the second wave, six Lancasters from No. 97 Squadron led by Squadron Leader John Sherwood. Each aircraft carried four 1,000lb (450kg) bombs with 11-second delayed action fuses.

Leaving the English coast near Selsey Bill, they flew low over the Channel to cross the French coast near Trouville, and continued hugging the ground southwards for about 100 miles (160km) before turning east.

Diversionary attacks were planned to keep German fighters occupied, but

AUGSBURG RAID REPORT, EXTRACT

Aircraft attacking	Bombs dropped	Release height	Time at target	Results observed
8	14.3 tons	50/400ft (15/121ft)	1955/2015	Huge red flames seen. One aircraft claimed hits on main building; two others claim bombs in target area.

"Owing to poor light and low altitude, photographs lacked all essential detail. No bomb bursts are shown, but a large fire is seen probably in the city of Augsburg, and it is clear that at least one and probably all the aircraft passed directly over the target. A PR photograph taken on 25/4 reveals severe damage chiefly to the S end of the works. The main Diesel Assembly Shop has suffered heavy damage."

Above: Squadron Leader John Nettleton led the daring daylight raid on the U-boat engine factory at Augsburg, for which he was awarded the Victoria Cross.

LANCASTER SQUADRONS, OPERATION MILLENNIUM

Squadron	Base	Date of first operation
144	Waddington	3 March 1942
97	Woodhall Spa	20/21 March 1942
207	Bottesford	24/25 April 1942
83	Coningsby	29/30 April 1942
61	Syerston	5/6 May 1942
106	Coningsby	30/31 May 1942
50	Skellingthorpe	30/31 May 1942
		(one aircraft only)

Augsburg finally hove into sight, and the two remaining Lancasters of No. 44 Squadron detoured around some tall factory chimneys and commenced their bombing run. At this point Garwell's aircraft was hit by flak and, shortly after releasing his bombs, he had to slide the burning Lancaster on to the ground. Four of the seven crewmen aboard survived, to be taken prisoner. Nettleton's Lancaster alone escaped into the gathering gloom.

Minutes later, the first Vic of the second wave from 97 Squadron arrived to find a thoroughly alerted defence. Unlike Nettleton, Sherwood did not attempt to dodge around the factory chimneys, but climbed above them, his two wingmen pulling into line astern behind him. All three aircraft bombed accurately, but Sherwood's Lancaster was mortally hit by ground fire, and crashed in flames shortly after. By some miracle, Sherwood himself survived with only minor injuries.

Meanwhile, the final Vic, which had dropped back still further, now came racing in from the south. They were met by a storm of anti-aircraft fire, and all three were badly damaged. One blew up just as its bombs fell clear, but the other two got through. Wearily the survivors climbed into the darkening sky, one

these miscarried. Between 20 and 30 Messerschmitt 109s of JG.2 returning to base encountered the rear Vic of Nettleton's wave. Attacking, they quickly shot down all three before turning their attention to the leading trio. One more Lancaster went down and the others were damaged before the Germans, by now low on fuel and ammunition, broke off the running battle. The second wave, although only a few miles away, was not spotted.

At this point Garwell's aircraft was hit by flak

Nettleton and Flying Officer J. Garwell, the other survior of the first wave, bored eastwards on track for Munich until over the Ammer lake they swung north towards Augsburg, followed at a distance of about 10 miles (16km) by the No. 97 Squadron formation.

Below: Wellingtons were the most numerous bombers participating in Operation Millennium. However, they were soon to be phased out in favour of the Avro Lancaster. (via Flypast)

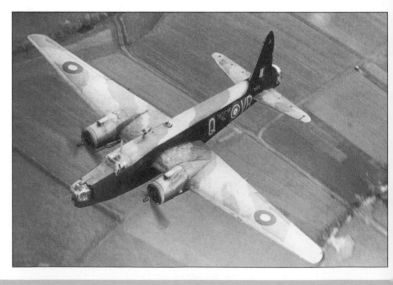

Above: No. 83 Squadron Lancasters took part in the 1,000 bomber raid on Cologne. This unit was also the first Lancaster Pathfinder squadron.

Right: Cologne at the end of the war, showing the devastation around the cathedral. Wrecked bridges block the Rhine.

with only three engines operative, and straggled back to base, where one of the surviving 97 Squadron aircraft was struck off charge.

Seventeen bombs hit the factory buildings, inflicting extensive damage on them. Nettleton was awarded the Victoria Cross for his exploit, and many other survivors were decorated for this, the first Lancaster raid to be made public. But with a loss rate exceeding 50 per cent it was not, by the very nature of things, repeatable, even though the interception by German fighters which had caused such havoc to the first wave had largely been a matter of ill fortune.

■ OPERATION ■ MILLENNIUM

By the end of May 1942, seven squadrons had Lancasters on strength. This was just in time for them to take part in a raid which for Bomber Command was a turning point in the night air offensive.

The strategic bombing of the Third Reich was, in its early days, an extremely haphazard affair, with individual crews plotting their own courses and timings. Navigation was inexact, and only one crew in three managed to place their bombs within 5 miles (8km) of the target. Any damage caused was a mere pinprick. To make matters worse, the German night fighter defences had taken the measure of this form of attack, and losses were steadily rising. Bomber Command's future looked increasingly uncertain. This was the situation when Air Marshal Arthur Harris assumed command in February 1942.

Harris realized that only a spectacular success could save his command from being broken up. Previous raids had neglected the cardinal principle of concentration of force. This had to be corrected. An unprecedentedly heavy raid on a single target was needed, concentrated in time and space. A raid by 1,000 bombers would be the biggest raid ever attempted; the magic number of 1,000 would attract interest and demonstrate that RAF Bomber Command was truly a force to be reckoned with.

The target chosen was Cologne. The city was within range of a new radio navigational device called Gee, and on a moonlit night the serpentine coils of the Rhine made it easily identifiable from

> **All aircraft would follow the same route from a merge point off the coast**

the air. To achieve concentration of force, all aircraft would follow the same route from a merge point off the coast (the first use of the bomber 'stream'), and the entire attack was to last just 90 minutes, an average of more than 11 aircraft bombing every minute! The German defences would

Above: Mk I R5609 flew with No. 97
Squadron on the Cologne and Essen
thousand-bomber raids. Later it took part
in the Battles of the Ruhr, Berlin, Hamburg
and Peenemunde. It survived the war.
(Alfred Price)

be saturated by weight of numbers, minimizing losses.

The Cologne raid took place on the night of 30/31 May 1942. The attack was in three waves, the first consisting of Gee-equipped Wellingtons and Stirlings with selected crews; their task was to locate the target and start fires to guide the main force in. The second wave consisted of the remaining Stirlings and Wellingtons, and the other twin-engined types – Hampdens, Whitleys and Manchesters. The third and most concentrated wave consisted of the new heavy bombers; more than 125 Halifaxes and about 75 Lancasters were scheduled to be over the target during the final 15 minutes of the attack. It has been suggested that this was to maximize the devastation in an already hard-hit city, but the fact is that operationally it was the best place for them. As the fastest and most heavily armed aircraft in the force, they were the least vulnerable to German night fighters, and equally were least likely to straggle on the homeward leg. This was borne out by events; losses to the third wave amounted to a mere 1.9 per cent, compared with 4.8 per cent to the first wave and 4.1 per cent to the second.

Post-war analysis by German generals described the Cologne raid as 'alarmingly effective'. For Bomber Command, it opened a new era in strategic bombing, with marked targets and highly concentrated attacks. Within three years, Lancasters would make up virtually the whole of the raiding force, and the damage they wrought upon German industry and communications was incalculable. From the Cologne raid onward, the history of the Lancaster was inextricably bound up with the development of Bomber Command's strategy and tactics.

The secret of success for Operation Millennium had been the ability to find the target and mark it for the following crews. While Gee was a useful navigation aid, it not only lacked the accuracy needed for blind bombing, but was too short-ranged to cover many important targets. The idea was mooted of a special target-finding force, and this was eventually formed in July 1942.

■ THE PATHFINDERS ■

Competition promotes increased efficiency, and Bomber Command introduced this in the form of a photographic ladder. It became standard procedure for each bomber to photograph its aim point, and each squadron's position on the ladder was determined by the accuracy of these. The ladder indicated which squadrons (and also which crews) were consistently finding their targets.

The first proposal was to form one or more elite units with selected crews.

For various reasons this was abandoned, and Path Finder Force (PFF) was formed, commanded by Group Captain Don Bennett, an Australian navigation expert and pre-war trailblazer.

Bomber Command was divided into operational areas called Groups. The squadron heading the photographic ladder in each of the four Bomber Groups was transferred to the newly formed No. 8 Pathfinder Group, based on Huntingdon. Inevitably, one Lancaster squadron was among them, No. 83. The others flew aircraft representative of the Groups in which they normally operated, but this was not to last. No. 156 Squadron traded its Wellingtons for Lancasters in January 1943; No. 7 Squadron its Stirlings in July of the same year, and finally No. 35 Squadron its Halifaxes in April 1944. By the end of the war, there were 14 Lancaster-equipped PFF Squadrons. But this was still three years in the future.

The first loads to go down contained a high proportion of incendiaries

Regrettably, PFF did not manage to bring about an instant improvement in bombing effectiveness. This had to wait for new navigational devices, for special pyrotechnic markers, and the development of methods which made the best use of them.

The former duly arrived in the shape of Oboe, an accurate but range-limited radio bombing device carried by Mosquitos. Dependent on signals from ground transmitters in England, it took in the highly industrilized Ruhr area, but not much else.

The heavy bombers were fitted with H2S, a radar navigation and blind bombing aid, although initially only a few aircraft carried it. It was much less accurate than Oboe, but as it was not dependent on external aids, it was not range-restricted.

Parachute flares had long been used as an aid to target finding. They had,

Above: Flak bursts punctuate the night sky over Germany as Pathfinder markers go down on a target. Two other bombers are just visible.

however, two drawbacks. Unless visibility was good, they would not light up the ground sufficiently well for crews to visually identify a target, or even pinpoint their own location. Then, of course, unless the flares were released in the right area, they simply illuminated a strange and often unrecognizable area of Germany, which was not a lot of help. Used in conjunction with Oboe or H2S, flares became far more effective.

In Operation Millennium, the first loads to go down contained a high proportion of incendiaries to start fires that would lead the following bombers to the target area. Something more accurate was needed, and this duly arrived in the form of markers, known as Target Indicators, or TIs.

Each TI contained 60 pyrotechnic candles. A barometric fuse preset to operate at low altitude blew the TI open, cascading the candles on to the ground, igniting as they went. Seen from above, the contents of each TI would appear as an intense pool of light, about 900ft (275m) in diameter. Burning time was about three minutes, so they needed to be replenished at frequent intervals.

By now the Germans had started to produce dummy targets to mislead the bombers. Their obvious reaction to TIs was to copy them and, when a raid was imminent, set them off on a dummy target. To circumvent this, TIs were produced in a combination of colours; red, yellow, green etc, and used in a predetermined order which varied from raid to raid.

When cloud covered the target, sky markers were used. These were parachute flares in a variety of colours, and sometimes throwing off coloured stars. Dropped by Oboe or H2S aircraft, they demanded a rather complicated offset bombing technique. While skymarking was nowhere near as accurate as ground marking, it gave accuracy far superior to the early years of the war, when 'agricultural bombing' – the accidental bombing of fields – was a common occurrence.

With the new equipment available, all that remained was to find the best methods of employing it. Oboe Mosquitos were used for the initial marking of all targets within its range. Outside Oboe reach, H2S was used. Tactics were roughly as follows. The first aircraft to arrive, typically five minutes before the main attack was scheduled to start, were the Finders, backed by a few Supporters. The Finders dropped flares where they thought the aiming points were likely to be. Having visually identified the aim point, they would drop further flares directly above it.

The Finders would be followed by the Illuminators, who would drop sticks of flares directly across the aim point. Then would come the Primary Markers, to put TIs on the aim point itself. Backers-Up would continue to drop TIs at intervals, to give the Main Force an aiming point throughout the attack.

This form of visual marking was code-named Newhaven. When, due to poor visibility or broken cloud, the marking was carried out using H2S, it became Parramatta, while skymarking was dubbed Wanganui.

Below: Flak damage sustained by a Lancaster of No. 50 Squadron over Leipzig. Miraculously, nothing vital was hit.

As with all new methods, teething troubles occurred, mainly due to the precise timing required. The first real success achieved by PFF came during the Barmen-Wuppertal raid on 29/30 May 1943. The target was accurately marked, and the subsequent bombing highly concentrated. How was this done?

■ BARMEN/WUPPERTAL ■

A total of 719 aircraft were despatched. Of these, 272 were Lancasters (the force had been building up rapidly, and a further 12 squadrons now operated the type). Of these, 20 aircraft were Lancaster Is and IIIs of PFF, and the attack was spearheaded by 11 Mosquito IVs fitted with Oboe.

Main Force, following on behind, included 31 Lancaster Is and IIIs of No. 8 Pathfinder Group; 76 Lancaster Is and IIIs of No. 1 Group; 16 Hercules-engined Lancaster IIs of No. 3 Group; and 129 Lancaster Is and IIIs of No. 5 Group. Loads consisted of a mixture of high explosives – 4,000lb (1,800kg) cookies in the case of the Lancasters, and incendiaries.

The bombing was heavy and concentrated

Visibility in the target area was poor, due to industrial haze and smoke, but the first Mosquitoes marked accurately at 00.47 hours, with red target indicators. They were followed by PFF backers-up with green TIs, and PFF 'fire-raisers' with incendiaries. Four of these, equipped with H2S, also marked with yellow TIs. Main Force aircraft were instructed to aim at the reds if visible; otherwise at the centre of the greens.

The bombing was heavy and concentrated; 611 aircraft claimed to have bombed the primary target. A total of 33 aircraft were lost on this raid, about 4.6 per cent. Lancaster losses amounted to seven, or about 2.6 per cent of those despatched; barely half the average losses for the raid.

A factor common to all forms of warfare is confusion, and the Pathfinder-led attacks on Germany were no exception. If a Pathfinder put down his TIs in the wrong place, for whatever reason, inevitably a proportion of Main Force would use them as an aim point. In addition, the Germans, by dint of much practice, grew adept at decoys. A third factor was creep-back; the tendency of crews over a heavily defended target to release their bombs at the earliest possible moment, with the result that the Main Force bomb pattern would extend further and further back from the original aim point until in extreme cases it ended in open countryside. What was

Above: **Incendiary bomb containers are loaded. Fires on the ground drew other bombers like moths to a candle.**

needed was a raid controller to direct the marking, giving a continuous running commentary on which TIs were to be used for aiming and which should be ignored; which was the real target and which a decoy; and generally keeping the bombing pattern tidy.

A possible solution appeared to be that pioneered by Wing Commander Guy Gibson for Operation Chastise, the destruction of the Mohne and Eder Dams in the Ruhr. He controlled his force, albeit a small one, very effectively using VHF voice radio to communicate. Possibly a Master Bomber could control an orthodox raid in the same way. There was only one way to find out – lay on a small-scale experiment.

■ OPERATION ■ BELLICOSE

An easy target would have proved little; in the event, the one chosen called for a high degree of precision. Friedrichshafen lies on the north shore of the Bodensee (Lake Constance), the south shore of which is in Switzerland. In the 1914–18 war it had been notorious as the home of the Zeppelin factory, a building complex about 1,500ft (460m) long by 1,050ft (320m) wide. In 1943, it was the largest production centre for radar parts in the whole of the Third Reich, and its destruction would be a severe blow to the German air defences, and much else.

EXTRACT FROM BOMBER COMMAND NIGHT RAID REPORT NO. 340

"611 aircraft, out of a force of 719, attacked the Barmen district of Wuppertal with very great success. The fire-raising technique was effectively employed, as a complement to ground marking, resulting in the best concentration yet achieved by the Pathfinder Force. Immense damage was caused in the town, covering over 1,000 acres and affecting 113 industrial concerns, as well as totally disrupting the transport system and public utilities."

Continuous marking of such a small target was next to impossible. Special tactics were needed. Main Force crews were to orbit the target at between 4 and 6 miles (6–10km), with no more than two aircraft at the same altitude. The instant a TI landed on the target, the Master Bomber would issue a special signal, and as many aircraft as possible would attack immediately. It was of course possible that the target could quickly become obscured by smoke; in this case, the crews were to make their attack run from a certain point, sighting on a second point, but delaying bomb release long enough for the aircraft to cover 6,000ft (1,800m) to the actual target.

This raid was sufficiently different for special training and picked crews to be needed. No. 5 Group supplied 56 Lancaster IIIs with experienced crews drawn from 12 squadrons. No. 8 Group provided four hand-picked Pathfinder crews from 97 Squadron, based at Bourn, also with Lancaster IIIs. Piloted by Flight Lieutenants

Rodley, a survivor of the Augsburg raid, and John Sauvage, and Pilot Officers D.I. Jones and Jimmy Munro, the latter a Canadian, they were flown north to Scampton for two days' intensive training.

It was perhaps significant that for this trial mission the Master Bomber was not a Pathfinder, but the very experienced Group Captain Leonard Slee. His deputy was the Australian squadron commander, Wing Commander G.L. Gomm. In addition, there were two controllers, either of whom could take charge in the event of an emergency. The force took off late in the evening of 20 June 1943 and headed south, crossing the Channel at maximum altitude. Once over France, they progressively lost height down to 10,000ft (3,050m) as they passed Orleans, then lower still to between 2,500 and 3,000ft (750–900m). After crossing the Rhine they began to climb to attack altitude, which was 5,000ft (1,500m) for the Pathfinders and 10,000ft (3,050m) for the Main Force. At about this time, Group Captain Slee's

Lancaster lost an engine and was unable to keep its place at the head of the stream. Wing Commander Gomm, of No. 467 (Australian) Squadron, took over as Master Bomber.

Exactly on time, Munro and Jones released a string of flares parallel to and on either side of the target. The gun defences opened up at once, more strongly than expected, and Gomm ordered all aircraft to gain another 5,000ft (1,500m). Realizing that this would make visual identification very difficult, the four Pathfinders stayed at their original altitude.

The Master Bomber ordered all aircraft to attack at once

Sauvage put down a green TI just north of thee Zeppelin sheds. He was followed by Rodley, who dropped a green TI accurately. On seeing this, the Master Bomber ordered all aircraft fitted with the Mk XIV bombsight to attack at once. An attempt to renew this marker failed. Jones later commented that he had to abandon one run because it was impossible to hold his aircraft steady in the concussions from the bombs. More flares were dropped along the shoreline

Below: Prototype Lancaster Mk III. Externally indistinguishable from the Mk I, the main difference was American-built Packard Merlins with Hamilton propellers.

Above: Aircraft of No. 50 Squadron at Swinderby. The nearest was struck off charge when it crashed at Thurlby, Lincolnshire, on 19 September 1942.

around the two predesignated points in order to enable the remainder of Main Force to bomb indirectly.

After the attack, all 59 Lancasters (one had been driven off track by thunderstorms) orbited the target to form up before heading for Maison Blanche and Blida airfields in Algeria, where they arrived safely.

For 'Rod' Rodley, however, it was an eventful trip. Unknown to him, a TI had hung up. When, far out over the Mediterranean he lost height, the barometric fuse operated and the candles ignited. The first intimation that all was not well came when an evil red glow suddenly appeared beneath his Lancaster. Thinking he was under attack from a night fighter, Rodley took evasive action, while Sergeant Duffy, his flight engineer, checked for damage. The bomb bay was a mass of flames, but the cause was obvious. A quick pull on the jettison toggle and the blazing remnants of the TI fell clear, leaving the Lancaster damaged but flyable.

Considerable destruction was caused to the target, and the Master Bomber concept was rated a success. Six of the Lancasters were damaged by anti-aircraft fire, one beyond repair. The 'shuttle'

concept of flying on to North Africa was also rated a success, and was later used by both Bomber Command and the USAAF. As a footnote, intercepts of German night fighter radio traffic revealed that patrols were flown in the Florennes/Juvincourt area, presumably waiting for the bombers to return. They did of course, several nights later, bombing La Spezia on the way for good measure.

As the strategic bombing of the Third Reich continued, PFF methods became ever more sophisticated, with contingency plans for almost every eventuality. At the same time, the proportion of Lancasters to other heavy bomber types grew ever greater. Moving forward in time to just over a year later, on 23/24 July 1944, a force of 619 heavy bombers was sent against the German naval base at Kiel. Of these, no fewer than 84 per cent were Lancasters.

■ PATHFINDER ■ PROGRESS

By this time, the concept of the Master Bomber was tried and proven. His function was to check on the accuracy of the marking, call by radio for adjustments or back-up where necessary, and, while loitering in the area until the bombing was completed, do everything possible to ensure that the munitions went down exactly where they were intended to go.

Whereas in the Friedrichshafen raid the Master Bomber had flown a Lancaster, loitering over heavily defended targets for extended periods in a four-engined bomber could not be considered a good insurance risk. It was not long before the standard aircraft for this purpose became the fast and agile twin-engined Mosquito. This was the case

BOMBER COMMAND AIRCRAFT IN RAID ON KIEL, 23/24 JULY 1944			
Group	**Type**	**No.**	**Missing**
8	Mosquito IX	1	–
	Mosquito XVI	6	–
	Mosquito XX	3	–
	Lancaster III	89	1
1	Lancaster I	85	1
	Lancaster III	104	1
6	Lancaster II	14	–
	Lancaster X	28	–
5	Lancaster I	46	1
	Lancaster III	53	–
3	Lancaster I	59	–
	Lancaster II	14	–
	Lancaster III	27	–
4	Halifax III	100	–
TOTAL			
10 Mosquitos, 519 Lancasters, 100 Halifaxes			

Top: To assist target identification, detailed models were made by the Central Intelligence Unit. Seen here is Kiel harbour.
Above: Lancaster Mk I of No. 83 Squadron. After a distinguished career with PFF, this aircraft came down in Holland after raiding Essen on 3/4 April 1943.

for the Kiel raid, in which the Master Bomber and his deputy flew two of the 10 Mosquitos allocated for primary marking. Some idea of PFF progress can be given by quoting the Plan of Attack in full.

"The method employed for the raid on Kiel was controlled Newhaven marking. Blind Illuminators, 21 Lancasters, were to drop red TIs at H-6 (six minutes before zero hour), and white flares if the weather was suitable. If there was more than 6/10ths cloud, they were to retain their white flares, and drop green flares with red stars instead. If their H$_2$S should prove unserviceable, they were to retain their markers and act as Main Force. These were to be followed by the Primary Visual markers, 6 Lancasters, at H-4, who were to drop red and green TIs using the red TIs dropped by the Illuminators as a guide, but only after definite visual identification. If they could not identify the target visually they were to retain their markers and act as Main Force. Visual Centerers, 16 Lancasters, distributed throughout the attack, were to aim green TIs with one second overshoot at: 1) the centre of mixed red and green TIs; 2) the centre of red TIs; 3) the centre of green TIs; in that order of priority. If no TIs were visible, they were to act as Main Force. The marking was to be kept up during the attack by the Secondary Blind Markers, 7 Lancasters at H+10 and 4 at H+II. They were to drop red TIs by H$_2$S. If there was more than 6/10ths cloud they were to release skymarking flares green with red stars. If their H$_2$S was unserviceable they also were to act as Main Force. 28 Lancasters of 8 Group were to act as supporters, bombing at H-6 on H$_2$S, or if that was unserviceable, visually or on a good dead reckoning."

■ KIEL ■

The Main Force was scheduled to attack in four very concentrated waves, putting 516 heavy bombers over the target in the space of just 15 minutes. Scattered among them would be 15 ABC (Airborne Cigar) Lancasters of No. 101 Squadron, each carrying an extra crewman whose function was to jam the German night fighter radio frequencies. Bombing instructions were, in order of priority: 1) centre of mixed red and green TIs or red TIs; 2) centre of green TIs; 3) centre of skymarking flares.

Rarely does anything go precisely according to plan, and the raid on Kiel was no exception. The target was covered with 10/10ths cloud. No contact could be made with the Master Bomber, and his deputy assumed control of proceedings. Marking was checked by H$_2$S and considered accurate, although rather scattered in the early stages. Main Force bombed on the glow of TIs as seen through the cloud, but both marking and bombing appeared to become more concentrated towards the end of the attack, and many explosions and fires were reported.

Severe damage was caused to the north-east portion of the Deutsche Werke shipyards, and hangars at the Holtenau airfield were partially destroyed. A considerable amount of damage was done to the facilities and barrack area near the Torpedo Boat Harbour, and moderate damage to a torpedo components and electrical signalling works. Sixteen medium-sized buildings in the Marine Artillery Depot were partially destroyed. Only four Lancasters were lost on this mission; a mere 0.7 per cent of the total.

PFF led the way to the targets, but Main Force, huge and largely anonymous, was the mighty sledgehammer that came crashing down on them.

For all practical purposes, Main Force was Bomber Command. Main Force delivered the greatest weight of bombs against the war machine that was the Third Reich, and Main Force took the greatest number of casualties. Nor should it be forgotten that Main Force was the training ground for those who became Pathfinders or who smashed the Ruhr Dams and sank the *Tirpitz*. Although it was occasionally diverted to tactical aims, by far the greatest effort was strategic.

As the war continued, the Lancaster progressively became the backbone of Main Force. In numbers of sorties flown and tonnages of bombs delivered, it outstripped all other bombers in service by a considerable margin.

The strategic bombing of Germany, and to a lesser extent its Axis partner Italy, consisted of a number of what amounted to protracted set-piece battles, interspersed with many highly individual actions. The thousand-bomber raids of May and June 1942 had only been achieved by milking training units of aircraft and crews, and pressing every possible reserve machine into service. This tremendous effort could not, by the very nature of things, be sustained. During the months following June 1942, Bomber Command restricted itself to raids of up to 300 aircraft against single targets roughly twice a week, weather permitting.

The number of Lancaster squadrons steadily grew. Prior to October 1942, conversion on to the new type was carried out by a specially formed third flight within each squadron. This allowed squadrons to operate old and new types side by side until conversion was complete, with them thus remaining fully operational. After this, conversion flights were centralized and merged into Heavy Conversion Units.

Top: Squadron crew returns from a raid. Two are Canadians and one a New Zealander, reflecting an ever-increasing influx from the Dominions.
Above: Wing Commander Guy Gibson (right) led No. 106 Squadron to Gdynia, dropped the first 8,000 pounder, and took part in Operation Robinson before forming the Dam Busters.
Far left: The devastated oil refinery at Harburg, just to the south of Hamburg.

Special weapons often feature in the Lancaster story. One of these was the huge Capital Ship Bomb, which featured a shaped charge designed to cut through armour. This monstrosity was turnip-shaped, and possessed appalling ballistic qualities for a role where accuracy was essential.

FRIEDRICHSHAFEN, BOMB LOADS

Leader and Deputy Leader	2 x Lancaster III	1 x 4,000lb (1,800kg) 7 x 500lb (227kg)
97 Sqn PFF	2 x Lancaster III	3 x red TI; 3 x green TI 16 x white flares 2 x 500lb (227kg) 2 x red TI, 2 x green TI 32 x white flares 2 x 500lb (227kg)
9, 49, 50, 57, 61, 106 Sqns, No. 5 Grp	32 x Lancaster III	1 x 4,000lb (1,800kg) 7 x 500lb (227kg)
44, 207, 467, 619 Sqns, No. 5 Grp	Lancaster III fitted with Mk XIV bombsight	14 x 500lb (227kg)
44, 207 Sqns, No. 5 Grp	Lancaster III not fitted with Mk XIV bombsight	Full incendiary load

SEARCHLIGHTS

"One of my most anxious moments of the whole raid was when, during one of my five successful runs over the target, T-Tommy was caught in a cone of searchlights. I fought desperately to lose those probing beams of light which had caught my aircraft in their web. Shrapnel rattled along the fuselage like hailstones until, by diving at near maximum speed, I escaped into the friendly darkness. Poor Jack Hannah, my wireless operator, stationed at the astrodome on the lookout for enemy fighters, protested in vigorous terms as he was tossed about like a pea in a pod."

PILOT OFFICER D.I. JONES, NO. 97 SQUADRON

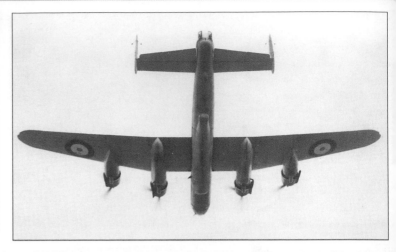

Targets for the Capital Ship Bomb were soon found. In August 1942, the German's only aircraft carrier *Graf Zeppelin* and the battle cruiser *Gneisenau* were reported at Gdynia in Poland. A raid was mounted on 27 August by Lancasters of No. 106 Squadron adapted to carry the special bomb. It was led by Wing Commander Guy Gibson, already possessed of a formidable reputation, with a specialist bomb aimer, Squadron Leader Arthur Richardson, for this mission only.

■ ANTICLIMAX ■

The result was, perhaps inevitably, an anticlimax. Visibility was poor, and the defences stronger than expected. Arriving over Gdynia, 106 Squadron was unable to locate *Graf Zeppelin*, but managed to find what was believed to be *Gneisenau*.

Top: To carry bombs of 8,000lb (3,600kg) or more, Lancaster bomb bay doors were bulged, as seen on this Mk II.

Above: A gaggle of Lancasters at low level. Not the Le Creusot raid, but these in Far Eastern finish show up much better.

Gibson made numerous runs over the harbour, and despite Richardson's best efforts, the bomb missed the battle cruiser by about 1,200ft (360m). The rest of the squadron fared no better. In the event, the German aircraft carrier never entered service.

Early in September, 8,000lb (3,600kg) bombs started to arrive on the squadrons. These needed bulged doors and other modifications to the bomb bay, and Gibson's squadron, its aircraft already adapted for the Capital Ship Bomb, pioneered their use. The following month saw another Bomber Command set-piece attack.

PARTICIPANTS IN OPERATION ROBINSON

Squadron	Number of aircraft	Base
9	10*	Waddington
44	9	Waddington
49	10	Scampton
50	12	Skellingthorpe
57	10	Scampton
61	7*	Syerston
97	9	Woodhall Spa
106	12*	Syerston
207	15	Langar

Denotes two aircraft to Montchanin.

Left: **Close examination reveals ice cream cornets among the bombs, denoting raids on *Dante's Daughter* of No. 103 Squadron. These symbolized Italian targets.**
Below: **Greetings from Canada! A tastefully decorated 8,000lb (3,600kg) bomb on its loading trolley in front of a Mk II of No. 426 Squadron RCAF.**
Bottom: **Lancaster Mk II of No. 426 Thunderbirds Squadron RCAF, one of the many Canadian Lancaster units. It was lost over Stuttgart on 7/8 October 1943.**

After take-off, on 17 October, some 96 Lancasters from 5 Group assembled in a loose gaggle over Upper Heyford in Oxfordshire, and from there proceeded to Land's End. Descending to 1,000ft (300m) over the sea to avoid radar detection, they gave Ushant a wide berth before turning south-easterly over the Bay of Biscay. When about 60 miles (95km) from the French coast, they dropped down to 300ft (90m) and turned almost due east.

Crossing the coast near the Isle d'Yeu, they swept over the sparsely populated Vendée, passed a few miles south of Tours, and picked up the River Cher at Montrichard. German fighters were absent, and unhindered by the defences, the low-level armada thundered on. The sole incident occurred as a Lancaster of No. 57 Squadron took a partridge through the windscreen, injuring the flight engineer.

■ OPERATION ■ ROBINSON

Vital targets were not always in Germany. One such was the Schneider armaments factory at Le Creusot in south-eastern France, roughly halfway between Dijon and Lyon. Although it covered nearly 300 acres, the need to avoid civil casualties demanded a standard of accuracy that could only be attained in daylight. The nine Lancaster squadrons operational in

No. 5 Group began to practise low-level flying early in October.

The lessons of the Augsburg raid had been well learnt. As in that ill-fated attack, the bombers were scheduled to reach the target just before dusk, making their escape into the darkening sky. This time, however, the inbound route of the raiding force was carefully planned to minimize the possibility of fighter interception.

4,000ft, the minimum release height for the 4,000lb cookies

Reaching the Loire near Nevers, the formation climbed to its briefed attack altitude of 4,000ft (1,200m), the minimum release height for the 4,000lb (1,800kg) cookies that were carried by 15 aircraft. As they climbed, they edged a few degrees southwards in the direction of Le Creusot and took up their attack formation.

Navigation and timing were spot on, and surprise

OVERSEAS LANCASTER SQUADRONS

Squadron	Nationality	First operation	Base
460	Australian	22/23 Nov 1942, Stuttgart	Breighton
467	Australian	2/3 Jan 1943, Gardening	Bottesford
426	Canadian	17/18 Aug 1943, Peenemunde	Linton-on-Ouse
405	Canadian	17/18 Aug 1943, Peenemunde	Gransden Lodge
408	Canadian	7/8 Oct 1943, Stuttgart	Linton-on-Ouse
432	Canadian	18/19 Nov 1943, Sea Search	East Moor
463	Australian	26/27 Nov 1943, Berlin	Waddington
75	New Zealand	9/10 April 1944, Villeneuve St George	Mepal
300	Polish	18/19 April 1944, Rouen	Faldingworth
419	Canadian	27/28 April 1944, Friedrichshafen	Middleton St George
428	Canadian	July 1944	Middleton St George
431	Canadian	December 1944	Croft
434	Canadian	2/3 Jan 1945, Nuremburg	Croft
424	Canadian	February 1944	Skipton-on-Swale
433	Canadian	1/2 Feb 1945, Ludwigshaven	Skipton-on-Swale
427	Canadian	11 March 1945, Essen	Leeming
429	Canadian	April 1945	Leeming

was virtually complete. The raiders arrived shortly after sunset, but the target was clearly visible despite the gathering dusk. In an attack lasting just nine minutes, over 200 tonnes of high explosive and incendiaries rained down.

At the same time, six Lancasters led by Guy Gibson broke away from the main force and attacked a transformer station at Montchanin, a few miles to the south-east. They carried ten 500lb (225kg) bombs each, and were briefed to attack from 500ft (150m). The transformer station was wrecked, but two of the pilots were over-enthusiastic and attacked from well below the minimum safe height. One aircraft was damaged and the other crashed, both victims of their own bomb explosions.

These were the only losses of the day, although one Lancaster forced to turn back with engine failure was intercepted by three Arado Ar 196 floatplanes of the Kriegsmarine. The flight engineer was killed in the attack, but the Lancaster gunners drove off the Germans, claiming two shot down.

In all, damage to the Lancasters was remarkably light, with just a few holes in some aircraft. Although limited production was resumed at Le Creusot after a period of about three weeks, major repair work was still in progress eight months later. Given the minimal casualties that were sustained, Operation Robinson must be reckoned an outstanding success.

The battle of El Alamein commenced just five days after the raid on Le Creusot, while Operation Torch, the Allied landings in north-west Africa, were scheduled for 11 November. Lancaster squadrons played an indirect part in these operations by bombarding targets in northern Italy, keeping the Italian Navy in port, and other reinforcements at home. Between 22/23 October and 11/12 December, 936 sorties were

Above left: The projection at the bottom of the turret is the Monica aerial; the damage was caused by flak.
Left: Star of Wings of Victory Week in Trafalgar Square, this No. 207 Squadron Lancaster was one of the first production aircraft. It survived the war.

flown. Genoa was raided five times, Turin seven times, and Milan once, this last in daylight. Italian air defences were ineffective and losses were light, even though France was often crossed in daylight on the outbound leg. But the long distances involved, plus a double crossing of the Alps, all carried out in late autumn weather frequently with icing conditions, made raiding Italy a tremendous test of endurance for the Lancaster crews.

If the weather was too bad for the Alpine crossing to be attempted, German targets were substituted instead at the last moment, causing, as Guy Gibson recorded, "Last minute flaps, a new briefing, a new maps, and bad tempers all round." Hamburg, Duisburg, Stuttgart and Mannheim were among the German targets attacked during this period.

Lancaster output soon reached the stage where squadrons from No. 1 Group, based in North Lincolnshire and South Yorkshire, could start equipping with the type. The first three to do so were No. 460 (Australian) Squadron at Breighton; No. 101 Squadron at Holme-on-Spalding Moor, the first operation of which was the long haul to Turin on 20/21 November; and No. 103 Squadron at Elsham Wolds.

The conversion of the Australian squadron on to the Lancaster highlighted a trend. Although No. 44 Squadron had been dubbed 'Rhodesia', there were not enough Rhodesians to man it fully. Of the 48 aircrew on the Augsburg raid, only eight were Rhodesians. Two, including Nettleton himself, were South Africans. Two Canadians, two New Zealanders and a single Australian completed the overseas contingent. The remaining 33 were British.

From the outbreak of war, volunteers from the British Empire, or Commonwealth, as it is now called, had hastened to the aid of the mother country. Their governments followed suit, and from quite an early stage, squadrons with national affiliations were formed. It is doubtful whether the personnel of these units was ever drawn entirely from just one country, but a high proportion of Australians, Canadians or New Zealanders in one squadron gave it a uniquely national flavour. No. 460 was the first of many such Lancaster squadrons, but numerically the Canadians took pride of place; No. 6 Group was for all practical purposes an all-Canadian Bomber Group.

■ ELECTRONIC ■ WARFARE

The year of 1943 commenced with raids on Berlin, with the Pathfinders honing their marking techniques on the city. Electronic warfare took on greater significance with the introduction of new jamming and threat detection systems. Of these, Tinsel could be tuned to transmit engine noise on the German fighter control frequencies; Monica was a tail warning radar; while Boozer could detect German radar emissions. Many other systems followed in the years to come.

Tinsel was initially successful, though the Germans gradually introduced measures to limit its effectiveness. Monica, in contrast, was a minor disaster from the outset. Quite unable to discriminate between friend and foe, it constantly gave false alarms as friendly aircraft in the bomber stream blundered into and out of its search area. Worse still, the Germans developed a detector codenamed Flensburg, which could home on Monica's emissions from very long ranges. Naxos-Z was another German detector, designed to home on H2S. The latter would have been no great problem had H2S been used intermittently for navigation, and for blind bombing in the target area, but many crews kept it switched on throughout the sortie,

Above right: Lancaster Mk 1 of No. 106 Squadron damaged by a night fighter during the Battle of the Ruhr in April 1943.
Right: Danger came not only from the air. This Lancaster collided on the ground with an American B-17 Fortress.

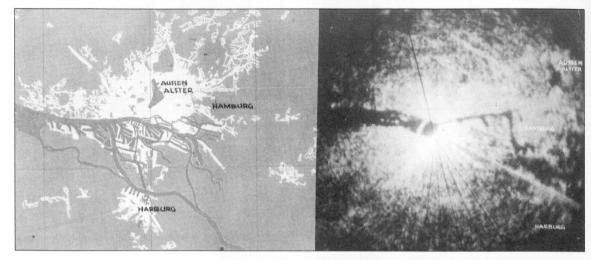

Above: Hamburg, with the distinctive River Elbe running through it, showed up well on the H2S screen, as can be seen by comparing it with the map at left. (Alfred Price)

making the task of the night fighters much easier.

Boozer, however, was rather better; if the bomber was illuminated by ground radar, a red warning light came on in the cockpit. If fighter radar emissions were detected, an orange light glowed. There were two snags. Illumination by ground radar was too frequent for the warning to be of much value, while once a night fighter gained visual contact its radar was often switched to standby, upon which the warning light went out precisely at the moment of greatest danger.

WINDOW OVER HAMBURG

Many references to the difficulties caused by Window to the ground and fighter defences were overheard in intercepted wireless traffic. Some enemy aircraft reported interference. One very interesting remark was "it is impossible, too many hostiles". This indicates that the Window echoes, besides producing general interference of the (German) display tube, were also confused with true aircraft echoes.

"115 sorties by night fighters were overheard, 33 of which mentioned British aircraft. Our crews reported 49 interceptions, but only seven of these developed into attacks. Enemy aircraft frequently seemed unaware of the presence of bombers in their vicinity. Only two instances of fighter damage were reported, and all of the five bombers seen to be shot down in combat were at least 20 miles (32km) away from Hamburg."

BOMBER COMMAND NIGHT RAID REPORT NO. 383

Below: Centurion! This 550 Squadron Lancaster survived the war with a tally of over 100 sorties against targets, which included the Ruhr and Berlin.

◼ THE BATTLE ◼ OF THE RUHR

The Ruhr was the industrial heart of Germany, invariably heavily cloaked by industrial haze, making targets notoriously difficult to locate. However, with the introduction of Oboe it could be attacked accurately for the first time.

The Battle of the Ruhr opened on 5/6 March with a heavy raid on Essen, the home of the Krupps steelworks, one of the most important targets in Germany. It was marked by PFF, then bombed by Main Force in three waves. The final wave consisted of 145 Lancasters from 14 squadrons, about half the Main Force total. One-third of the Krupps works was heavily damaged, more than all previous raids on this target combined had achieved.

Raids on Munich, Nuremberg and Stuttgart followed, to avoid setting a pattern which would allow the defences to concentrate, then, just over a week later, Bomber Command returned to Essen. A third raid on Essen took place on 3/4 April, and a fourth on 30 April/ 1 May. Barmen/Wuppertal, described in the preceding chapter, also fell into this period. Another Ruhr target, Duisburg, had been raided twice. Dortmund and Dusseldorf were hit during May with over 300 Lancasters on each raid, the first time this figure had been exceeded. Raids on targets in the Ruhr continued until 14/15 June, culminating in a heavy attack on the steel and coal centre of Oberhausen.

The Battle of the Ruhr conclusively demonstrated Bomber Command's ability to hit targets in this area even in poor visibility, while taking only moderate casualties. But the Ruhr was within range of Oboe. The pressing need was to carry the battle deeper into Germany with similar results.

■ OPERATION GOMORRAH ■

Hamburg was the second largest city in Germany, and the largest port in Europe. Its strategic importance lay in its shipbuilding activities, most notably the manufacturing of U-boats. Situated close to the coast, and with a large and very easily recognizable river running through it, Hamburg was suitable for locating by H_2S.

In addition, a new counter-measure codenamed Window was made available for the first time. It consisted of bundles of aluminium foil strips, which would each give the appearance of a heavy bomber on German radars, making tracking impossible.

On the night of 24/25 July 1943, 791 bombers set course for Hamburg. Of these, 347, or slightly less than half, were Lancasters, but they carried nearly three-quarters of the total tonnage of bombs. As they approached, they were monitored by German ground radar until the bomb aimers started to drop bundles of Window down their flare chutes at one-minute intervals.

Above: Time exposure of German flak over a defended area. This is what the Lancaster crews faced nightly.
Right: Flight Lieutenant William Reid VC of No. 61 Squadron. Twice wounded, his aircraft badly damaged and two crewmen dead, he continued the mission and bombed the target.

The result was complete chaos for the defenders. One minute they could see many contacts, indicating a heavy raid was underway. The next, the radar screens filled up, giving the appearance of a raid by 11,000 bombers! All semblance of control was lost, and fighters already airborne were ordered to the vicinity to hunt independently. They spent most of their time fruitlessly chasing clouds of Window, while the flak was reduced to firing at random, in the hope of scoring a lucky hit.

PFF marked accurately with Newhaven, and Main Force, now virtually unhampered by the defences, sent their bombs whistling down. Bombing accuracy was marred only by an element of 'creepback' in the later stages, caused by over-eager crews releasing their bombs a fraction too early on the attack run. Cumulatively, this extended for 7 miles (11km).

The loss rate for Hamburg had previously been around 6 per cent, but on this night only 12 aircraft were missing, a rate of 1.5 per cent. Only four Lancasters failed to return, but three of these were from the high-flying No. 103 Squadron, which had gained the least protection of all from Window.

■ FOLLOW-UPS ■

Hamburg's ordeal was far from over. Daylight raids by the USAAF 8th Air Force were made on 25 and 26 July, while on the night of 27/28, Bomber Command returned in force with 787 aircraft, 353 of them Lancasters. The same tactics were used, and losses were still very light at 2.2 per cent. A third raid followed on 29/30 July, and the fourth and final one on 2/3 August. The damage assessment report stated: "The city of Hamburg is now in ruins. The general destruction is on a scale never before seen in a town or city of this size."

The next event of note was a heavy raid upon the weapons research centre at Peenemunde. This was a high-risk mission; Peenemunde was a small target on the Baltic coast, and good visibility was needed for bombing accuracy, so much so that a full-moon night was chosen, 17/18 August. Deep penetrations were seldom made at this time of year, as the northern sky was never completely dark. Conditions were therefore ideal for the night fighters.

The force despatched consisted of 324 Lancasters, 219 Halifaxes and 54 Stirlings, with Group Captain John Searby of No. 83 Squadron as Master Bomber. The course to the target was planned to make it look as if the bombers were heading for Berlin. This impression was reinforced by eight PFF Mosquitos, which carried out a diversionary attack. It worked, and over 200 German fighters converged on the capital. But once bombs started going down on

Top left: Most Lancasters died in flames, as did this Heavy Conversion Unit aircraft following a training accident.
Left: Lancaster Mk I ME703 of No. 576 Squadron survived the holocaust of the Nuremburg raid in March 1944, only to receive a direct flak hit five weeks later.
Below: Chaos in the Juvissy marshalling yards after a raid by 200 Lancasters on 18/19 April 1944.

In what amounted to a short campaign, some 3,095 sorties were flown, 1,373 of them by Lancasters. In total, more than 8,600 tons of bombs fell on Hamburg, of which Lancasters alone contributed over 6,000 tons. Losses were 86 bombers, 39 of them Lancasters. Apart from the damage inflicted on the target, the German defence system, fire and rescue services had been left in complete disarray.

The defenders proved more resilient than expected. Measures taken included a looser form of fighter control, new airborne radar of a different wavelength, emission detectors as described earlier, and saturating the target area with 'cat's-eye' single seaters. Before long, bomber losses started to rise again.

Top: This Canadian Lancaster visited Berlin on at least seven occasions, flying with three different squadrons: Nos. 432, 426 and 408. *Above:* Casualty! Shot down over Berlin, this Lancaster broke up in mid-air and its taillanded in a garden. (Alfred Price)

PFF marking was not up to scratch, and the bombing was scattered. The absence of a Master Bomber did not help matters. Four days later they tried again, this time with better results.

A further 11 heavy raids on the German capital were carried out by the middle of February, interspersed with other targets. Results were indeterminate; while at first losses were light, they gradually increased. In all, 6,209 Lancaster sorties were flown in this period, losing 321 aircraft in action. This represented an unsustainable loss rate of 5.2 per cent, which rose to 8 per cent for a final raid in March

Peenemunde was heavily damaged, but the price was high

These figures do not include operational attrition. Fog and low cloud over England in the small hours of 17 December caused the loss of 28 Lancasters, in addition to 25 missing, while two more had collided after takeoff. The loss rate for this one mission was an appalling 11.4 per cent.

The success of Hamburg could not be repeated. Berlin was too large an area, too heavily defended, too far inland, and much harder to indentify with any precision. By this time, the advantages of Window were much less, as the German defences adapted themselves to it. While extensive damage was caused, the concentrated destruction of Hamburg was not repeated.

■ NUREMBERG ■

If the Battle of Berlin was a defeat for Bomber Command, the raid on Nuremberg on 30/31 March 1944 was a disaster. For Bomber Command, the Nuremberg raid was the night when it all went wrong.

Deception attacks on Kassel and Cologne were recognized early, which enabled the defences to concentrate on

Peenemunde, there was no disguising the real target, and those fighters with sufficient fuel stormed north to intercept, arriving in time to encounter the final two waves.

Peenemunde was heavily damaged, but the price paid for the raid upon it was high. Losses amounted to 40 aircraft, of which 24 were Lancasters. It is believed that the majority fell to

fighters, but how much worse this could have been had the fighters not been lured elsewhere first. Diversions and feints became a standard tactic in Bomber Command's armoury, followed later as strength increased by simultaneous attacks on multiple targets.

■ THE BATTLE ■ OF BERLIN

The operations so far described were successful, but Bomber Command also had setbacks. The Battle of Berlin was one such. It commenced on 18/19 November 1943 with an attack by an all-Lancaster force, but on this occasion

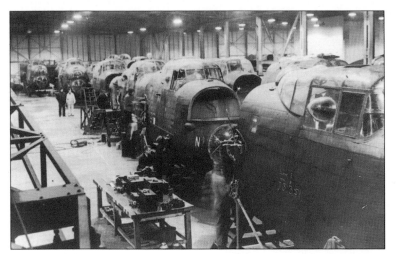

half moon. The track of the bombers was visible from miles away, and the fighters needed no further invitation.

94 bombers failed to return that night, while 13 crashed on their return

An incredible total of 94 bombers failed to make the return journey from Germany that night, while 13 crashed on their arrival at base. Yet another was written off with battle damage, for an attrition percentage of 13.83. Seventy more aircraft returned with varying degrees of damage.

Most of the losses occurred on the outward leg. Night fighters accounted for 78 aircraft, including 55 Lancasters; flak claimed 11 (five of them Lancasters); two bombers collided and another was lost to an unknown cause. Of the 440 Lancaster crewmen who failed to return home, only 107 survived. Worst of all was that the raid was an almost complete failure.

Top left: The remains of the V-weapons site at Wizernes after a raid by Lancasters of No. 5 Group, 20 July 1944.
Left: Repair was a vital part of aircraft replacement. The nearest fuselage section belonged to an aircraft badly damaged by a night fighter in June 1944.
Below left and right: Before and after. A raid on the oil storage depot at Bec d'Ambes on 4 August 1944.

the main raid of 781 heavy bombers, of which 569 were Lancasters from 34 different squadrons. The twin-engined night fighters were scrambled and ordered to assemble over a certain radio beacon. Unfortunately, the course of the bombers took them towards this beacon, running them straight into the trap. Forecast winds were incorrect, and the bomber stream became spread out. Then, by mischance, atmospheric conditions were such that long condensation trails formed behind the bombers, shining white in the clear air under a

■ RETURN TO EUROPE ■

The outcome of the entire war in Europe hinged on the successful invasion of Normandy. From April 1944, the majority of Lancaster sorties were against targets in France and Belgium, mainly railway centres and airfields, radar stations and coastal gun batteries.

The weeks following D-Day saw Main Force heavily engaged in France and the Low Countries. Road and rail communications, enemy troop concentrations and fuel depots were all accorded priority, but meanwhile the V-l and V-2 assault on London had begun, and a great deal of effort was diverted to their launching sites. Nor were targets in the Third Reich neglected; the Germans could be given no opportunity to move their home defence fighters forward.

This period saw a large-scale return to daylight operations for Bomber Command, made possible by Allied air superiority in the area, although the need to keep up the pressure around the clock made great demands on the bomber crews. Then, as the Allied armies pushed further inland, heavy attacks were made on German-held airfields in Holland. As the German defences were ground down, losses became progressively lighter; barely 1 per cent for December 1944.

During the concluding six months of the war, the Lancaster force grew to an

Above: Lancaster assembly line at Baginton. The wartime censor has rather clumsily airbrushed out the aircraft number.

enormous 57 squadrons; over 1,200 aircraft in all. As the area of occupied Europe shrank, so targets in Germany featured more and more. Concentrated attacks on synthetic oil plants were made during the winter of 1944/45, vastly reducing supplies. Dresden, at that time a key road and rail target, was attacked in strength on 13/14 February 1945; Essen by more

than 1,000 bombers in daylight on 11 March, and Kiel on 9/10 April. Berlin, once the most heavily defended area in Germany, was raided five nights later by more than 500 Lancasters, of which only two (0.4 per cent) failed to return. But by this time major targets were in short supply and the majority of raids were on a comparatively small scale, and as the Allied armies pushed into Germany, the strategic bombing war gradually drew to a close.

■ FINAL OPERATIONS ■

The Lancaster ended the war on more peaceful tasks. Operation Manna saw 17 Lancaster squadrons dropping containers of food to the population of Holland; Operation Exodus involved the repatriation of released British prisoners of war, with basic accommodation for 24 passengers in each aircraft. This was followed by Operation Dodge, the return of 8th Army veterans from the Mediterranean area. It was an honourable finish to a hard-fought campaign.

Left: Edith, veteran of 84 sorties during which she destroyed a German fighter, completed a further 14 trips dropping food and repatriating prisoners of war.

A heavily defended target could put up a storm of light flak, but most bombing was carried out at altitudes beyond its reach. Heavy flak could not be avoided by high flying, but it had a far slower rate of fire than the light automatic guns. Not only were far fewer shells coming up at any one time, but they took between 20 and 30 seconds to arrive at typical operational altitudes. Radar-predicted heavy flak was pretty accurate, but one method of avoiding it was to change course and altitude at frequent intervals. Hopefully the shells would then burst in the spot where the bomber would have been had it not evaded.

This improved the odds a bit, but if shells came up in the wrong place or burst at the wrong height, Lady Luck became the sole arbiter. Many pilots felt that the best course was to take no evasive action at all, but to drop the nose and accelerate out of the flak zone as fast as possible. It was also undesirable to make radical changes of course and altitude while on the attack run, if bombing accuracy was to be maintained. But having said that, the Lancaster's deadliest enemy was the fighter, whether met by day or by night. As the vast majority of Lancaster

sorties were made under cover of darkness, we will concentrate on the night fighter threat.

As we saw in the preceding chapter, countermeasures were widely used to hinder the defenders. While these were often very effective, what they could not do was prevent a fighter from searching visually. If a night fighter succeeded in working its way into the bomber stream, it was in a target-rich environment. Even with its radar and radio communications jammed solid, it was often possible for the fighter to make a visual sighting without these

Above: Radar-predicted heavy flak guns were mainly deployed along the coast or around cities.
Below left: Searchlights illuminated the bomber for flak or fighters; they could also dazzle the pilot and disorient him.
Opposite: Two .50 calibre machine-guns in the tail gave a mightier punch than the usual four .303 Brownings.

aids. And once the fighter was in visual contact, an attack usually followed.

Normal Lancaster defensive armament consisted of two machine-guns in each of nose and dorsal positions, and four more in the tail, all in power-operated turrets. The guns were Browning .303 calibre, with a high cyclic rate of fire. They could pour out a lot of rounds, but the bullets themselves were small and lacked hitting power. Four types of ammunition were in general use: ball, tracer, armour-piercing and incendiary.

The four guns in the rear turret were usually harmonized on a point at 750ft (225m) for night missions, and on a 7ft 6in (2.29m) square pattern at 1,200ft (365m) by day. The nose and mid-upper turrets were normally harmonized 5ft (1.52m) apart at 1,200ft (365m), although it was generally accepted that the maximum effective range of the .303 Browning was 900ft (275m). The main defence at night was the tail and

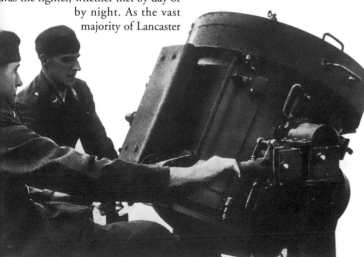

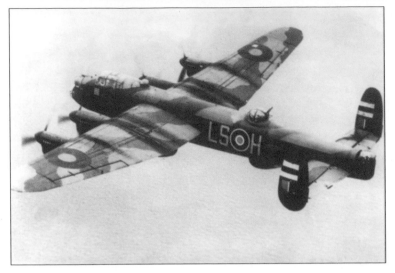

Left: The tail and mid-uper turrets were the Lancaster's main defensive armament. This example, from No. 15 Squadron, also carries G-H radar bombing equipment.
Below left: Mk I Lancaster used for traials of a periscopically sighted ventral turret in 1942. It was not a success.

into the effective range of the British machine-guns, which could to a degree compensate for their small projectiles by their high rate of fire.

From June 1944, a number of Lancasters were fitted with the Rose Rice tail turret, which mounted two .50 calibre Brownings. While the combination of a much heavier projectile and a slightly higher muzzle velocity gave a rather better effective range, the cyclic rate of fire of this weapon was at most 850 rounds per minute. The standard four-gun Lancaster turret could spew out no less than 306 bullets in a four-second burst, compared with just 113 for the Rose Rice turret. It must, however, be admitted that the weight of fire of the latter was about 50 per cent heavier provided that all bullets struck home, but the former was more likely to score multiple hits.

mid-upper turret, in that order. Rarely were the nights clear enough to allow fighters to make frontal attacks, and it was unlikely that a Lancaster would overhaul a fighter from astern, so the nose turret was of most use in discouraging the ground defences during low-level missions.

Wartime British bomber armament has often been criticized as inadequate, because it was both out-ranged and out-gunned by the German fighter weapons. There are, however, two factors

to consider: British bombers were far more heavily defended than those of any other nation except the Americans, and that included their German counterparts. For example, the Heinkel He 111 typically carried a single rifle-calibre machine-gun in each of just five positions, with limited fields of fire and no power-operated turrets. Then at night, visibility was such that the German fighters often had to get very close before they could see the bomber clearly enough to identify it and take aim. This brought them well

The primary task of the Lancaster was to deliver bombs and return safely

Operationally, what were the implications? The primary task of the Lancaster was to deliver bombs on target and return safely. Given this, it was sufficient to foil the fighter's attack. Shooting it down was the cherry on the cake. On dark nights, when the fighters were forced to get in close, sometimes to less than 200ft (60m), the four-gun turret, with nearly triple the rate of fire of the Rose Rice, had much to commend it. Few German night fighter pilots would press home an attack while they were taking hits themselves. The final advantage o

LANCASTER, DEFENSIVE GUNS

	.303 calibre	.50 calibre
Browning machine-gun		
Cyclic rate of fire	1,150rpm	750/850rpm
Weight	22lb (10kg)	64lb (29kg)
Muzzle velocity	2,660ft/sec (811m/sec)	2,750ft/sec (838m/sec)
Projectile weight	174 grains	710 grains

Above: The nose turret was rarely of use at night, but daylight raids became more frequent. No. 100 Squadron – 128 operations.

the standard four-gun turret was that it had no less than 130 seconds' firing time, compared with a mere 24 seconds for the Rose Rice. However, unless shooting up ground targets was on the agenda, this was rarely called for; against enemy fighters 24 seconds' firing time was usually adequate.

If, however, the object of the exercise was to shoot down German fighters, then the heavier gun was preferable. This was also the case on clear nights with good visibility, when the German fighters could stand off at long range and shoot. In daylight – and from late 1944 Lancaster carried out a surprising number of daylight operations – it was no contest; the heavier gun with its longer range was by far the most preferable. Among the squadrons equipped with the Rose Rice rear turret were Nos. 83, 101, 153 and 170.

The other major variation in Lancaster defensive armament was the Glenn Martin 250 mid-upper turret, which also mounted two .50 calibre Brownings. This was carried by the Lancaster B.VII, of which a total of 150 were built. But as deliveries of this model did not commence until April 1945, it was just too late to see action.

■ GUNSIGHTS ■

Guns are not a lot of use unless they can be accurately aimed. The main gunsight used in Lancaster turrets was the Barr & Stroud G Mk III reflector sight. In use, this showed an illuminated orange circle with a central dot, both focused at infinity. A brightness control adjusted it according to conditions: bright in sunlight, dim at night. The radius of the circle was approximately equal to the wingspan of a single-engined fighter at a range of 1,200ft (365m), while the radius of the circle gave the deflection (the amount of aiming ahead) needed to hit a target with a relative crossing speed of 50mph (80km/hr).

In 1944, the Mk IIc gyroscopic sight entered service as a turret sight. This could actually predict the point of aim, although only if the approaching fighter could be tracked for a short while, and its wingspan set on a dial. For this reason, it was very much a daylight sight, as it was rare for a gunner to have time to do such things at night. Finally, a gun-laying radar codenamed Village Inn was introduced in the final months of the war, which allowed opponents to be engaged from beyond visual range. While potentially devastating, the problem was obtaining positive identification of the radar contact as hostile. The means were to hand, but the war ended before unrestricted blind firing could be permitted as a general rule.

The essence of effective defence against fighters was always to see them first. At night this was far from easy.

ROSE RICE TURRET

2 x .50 Browing machine-guns
335 rounds per gun
Mk IIIA reflector sight
Traverse +/-94°
Elevation 49°
Depression 59°

Above: Mk I fitted with an experimental arrangement of remote barbettes with the sighting position in the tail.

As a general rule, they came from below, where they were masked by the dark ground and most difficult to see. By contrast, the bomber would be limned against the sky, which is always a fraction lighter, even on a starless night. Attacks generally came from astern, with the fighter swimming up from the depths and attacking in a slight climb with its fixed frontal armament. Its target was rarely the fuselage, as if the bombs detonated, the resulting explosion could quite easily destroy

Below: Canadian-built Mk X, fitted with the small and neat Glenn Martin mid-upper turret.

the night fighter too. Normally the wings, with the vulnerable engines and fuel tanks, were selected as the aiming point, although many a time silencing the rear gunner was a priority.

Later in the war, the German night fighters used Schrage Musik, cannon pointing upwards at an angle of about 60 degrees, aimed by a reflector sight mounted in the cabin roof. This allowed them to attack from almost directly underneath, out of the arcs of fire of all except those few Lancasters which had retained ventral turrets, and generally out of sight of the gunners also. All the fighter had to do was to formate beneath the bomber and take

careful aim at the fuel tanks between the engines. A short burst of fire was then usually sufficient.

■ SCHRAGE MUSIK ■

Because the German fighters did not use tracer in a Schrage Musik attack, Bomber Command was rather slow in identifying it. If a bomber set out, then failed to return, there was no one to tell the tale. Only those few aircraft that survived such attacks limped back bearing the tell-tale scars, and gradually the tactic became known.

Methods of dealing with night fighters varied. Often, if one was sighted that was not making any overtly aggressive moves, the policy was to leave it well alone, hoping that the bomber had not been seen. Other crews maintained that an aggressive attitude was best, opening fire even at long range in order to show the fighter the kind of welcome it could expect if it made an attacking move. Sometimes these ploys worked; at other times they didn't.

Flight Lieutenant Tony Weber's Pathfinder crew developed their own unique brand of defence against attack from below. The Lancasters of No 405 Squadron had had their dorsal turrets removed to improve performance, which left the mid-upper gunner as a spare bod. A small viewing hole was cut in the fuselage floor aft of the bomb bay, fitted with safety straps oxygen connection and power for a heated flying

Above: 'Village Inn' gunlaying radar was fitted to a few tail turrets towards the end of the war.

Left: The most widely used German night fighter was the radar-equipped Messerschmitt Me 110G.

The result was a steep descent right on top of the offending fighter, accompanied by the fervent hope that the German pilot's reflexes were fast enough for him to get out of the way in time. Negative 'g' made the Merlins cut through fuel starvation, temporarily extinguishing the exhaust flames and probably adding to the German pilot's visual problems. One dose of this nerve-racking treatment usually convinced him to go and look for someone who didn't play so rough. No. 405 Squadron later adopted the ventral viewing hole on all its aircraft.

The other, official counter to fighter attack was the corkscrew. Few people (and fighter pilots are no exception) are

suit. This position was then manned by the erstwhile mid-upper gunner. When a fighter was spotted coming in below, the pilot was warned. He immediately throttled back and lowered 10 degrees of flap, which killed a lot of speed and gave the aircraft greater manoeuvrability. As the Lancaster slowed, the fighter started to overshoot beneath it. Then, at the critical moment, Weber shoved the yoke fully forward, putting his huge bomber into a dive.

Above: The upward slanting cannon installation known as Schrage Musik allowed the night fighters to attack from the blind spot below the Lancaster. (Alfred Price)

any good at deflection shooting, and the object of the corkscrew was to give the fighter a difficult target rather than a sitting duck.

It consisted of a steep turn of about 30 degrees combined with a dive of about 500ft (150m), followed immediately by a steep turn of about 30 degrees in the opposite direction combined with a climb of about 500ft (150m). These manoeuvres would be repeated as long as the fighter was in an attacking position. In this way, course and altitude could both be maintained, at the expense of speed over the ground, while few German fighter pilots were good enough to follow a

corkscrewing Lancaster and still get into a good firing position.

Instructions for the corkscrew were given by the man best placed to see what was happening – usually the rear gunner, although the mid-upper gunner or the bomb aimer, from a position in the astrodome, could also act as controller for the engagement. On spotting a fighter moving into position, the man making the sighting would call over the intercom, "Prepare to corkscrew left [or right]", the rule being to break into the direction of the attack where possible. Then as the fighter moved into firing range, the executive order of "Go" would be given, launching the bomber into a series of wild gyrations. The controls had to be handled roughly, making the corkscrew violent, if it were to be really effective. The Lancaster could corkscrew very well

even with a 12,000lb (5,400kg) bomb on board, while unladen it was extremely manoeuvrable for such a large machine.

McLean was credited with five German fighters shot down plus one probable

Survival depended on teamwork – total co-operation and trust between pilot and gunners. A classic engagement occurred on 15/16 March 1944 following an abortive raid on an aero engine factory at Metz, near the Franco-German border.

The Lancaster was from No. 617 Squadron, the Dam Busters, and had a mainly Canadian crew. The rear gunner

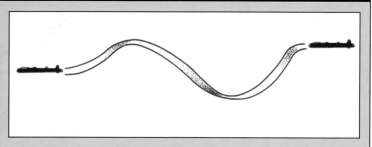

THE CORKSCREW MANOEUVRE

The corkscrew was a manoeuvre designed to make it very difficult for an enemy fighter to gain a firing position.

Above: Some Lancaster squadrons removed their dorsal turrets to improve performance.

up a contact to port at a range of about 3,600ft (1,100m). McLean strained his eyes, finally making out a dark shape which appeared to be four-engined. At first it was assumed to be another returning bomber. Gradually the shape closed, which was unusual, and when it was about 2,700ft (820m) away, McLean realized that it was actually two night fighters in close proximity to one another. Following standard procedure, he told his pilot: "Prepare to corkscrew port!"

■ THREE FIGHTERS ■

The next shock came quickly; a Messerschmitt 109 single-seater fighter was sighted, flying abreast of the Lancaster about 1,500ft (450m) distant with navigation lights burning! The only explanation for this behaviour seemed to be that it was trying to distract the gunners from the fighters astern. At this moment, one of the two broke towards the Lancaster with obviously aggressive intentions.

As it closed, McLean gave the order "Go!" and Duffy commenced a violent corkscrew just as the fighter opened fire at extreme range. The Lancaster was hit, but not seriously, and the German pilot broke away before lining up for another firing pass.

was a Scot with original ideas about defensive tactics, and only that morning the crew had been on a fighter affiliation exercise to try them out.

Men are born with differing abilities. Some have a natural flair for ball games; others play the piano outstandingly well. Flight Sergeant T.J. McLean's individual talent, and indeed his whole instincts, were for air-to-air gunnery. Credited with five German fighters shot down plus a probable on a previous tour of operations, he had volunteered to join No. 617 Squadron, widely regarded at that time as a suicide outfit, and had been assigned to Flying Officer Bill Duffy's crew as the tail gunner.

Past experience had convinced Tom McLean that the most effective loading

for his guns was 45 per cent tracer and 55 per cent armour piercing, rather than the ball, tracer, incendiary and armour-piercing mix laid down in regulations. On this trip he had unofficially arranged for his preferred mix to be loaded for the first time, to his rear turret only. Not even the crew knew about this; the nose turret and the mid-upper, which was manned by Canadian Red Evans, both had standard loadings.

All aircraft were recalled without bombing when it was found that the target was under heavy cloud, but on the return trip across France the sky was cloudless, the stars shone brightly, and visibility was exceptionally good.

The first warning came from Monica, the tail warning radar, which picked

Above: German night fighters were largely dependent on ground control to position them in the bomber stream.

Having drawn no return fire from the bomber, the Me 110 was more venturesome on its second attack, closing right in. Once again the big bomber corkscrewed, spoiling its aim, while McLean poured an angry burst of fire at it, hitting its port engine, then called "Drop" over the intercom. Immediately, the flight engineer throttled back all four engines and the Lancaster rapidly lost speed, reducing the range faster than the German pilot had expected, or was prepared for. McLean drew a bead on the cockpit and once more let fly. On hearing his guns, the flight engineer once more opened the throttles in what was a very well-rehearsed manoeuvre.

The second fighter plunged earthwards, trailing a comet-like fiery tail

On fire, the first Me 110 fell away into the void, and after making sure that the second fighter still remained in its original position, the rear gunner passed the word "Easy" over the intercom. Upon hearing this, Bill Duffy relaxed the corkscrew manoeuvre.

They were not left in peace for long. The second night fighter, made cautious by seeing the fate of its partner, moved out to a position almost abeam of the Lancaster before commencing a curving attack from slightly below it. Again, a violent evasive corkscrew, again a torrent of fire from both rear and mid-upper turrets, and the second fighter plunged earthwards, trailing a comet-like fiery tail.

Still the Me 109 shadowed them, just out of range. A renewed visual search (Monica had been switched off) showed yet another Me 110 coming up behind, moving from port to starboard, then finally to almost dead astern.

At this point Duffy spotted some cloud ahead and below, and pushed over into a shallow dive towards it. As he did so, the 110 came in, and once more the Lancaster went into a hard corkscrew, this time to starboard. Almost immediately McLean called "Drop!" The combination of corkscrew and speed loss spoiled the German pilot's aim completely, and he came hurtling in, to be met by a barrage of tracer and armour-piercing bullets at close range. With pieces flying off, his aircraft nosed up with flames bursting from its port wing and starboard engine, before entering a jerky flat spin down into the abyss. A red glow lit the cloud layer below.

At this, the Me 109 switched off its lights and turned in for an attack from abeam of the Lancaster. The tail turret could not be brought to bear, but Red Evans in the mid-upper position returned fire, then, as the Me 109 passed beneath

Below: In March 1944, a Lancaster of No. 617 Squadron accounted for three Me 110 night fighters like these in a single action. (Alfred Price)

the bomber, quickly traversed his turret to speed it on its way on the far side. It never returned.

At this stage of the war, night fighters were encountered quite frequently. Sometimes, by dint of hard manoeuvring or escaping into cloud, the bomber managed to shake them off. At other times, the air gunners managed to beat off the attack, while just occasionally they shot one down. In the general scheme of things, four against one was impossible odds; to survive such an encounter, let alone shoot down three fighters and beat off a fourth, bordered on the miraculous.

There are several footnotes to this outstanding action. As noted in the preceding chapter, Monica could be homed on from very long ranges. It was almost certainly this which drew as many as four fighters to a single Lancaster.

The corkscrew saved the lives of hundreds of bomber crewmen

The role of the Me 109 was more mysterious. Was it a deliberate decoy, or had it left its lights on accidentally? It seems hardly likely that it was acting as a controller, and it is extremely doubtful that it was acting as a station-keeping aid for the twin-engined fighters; they had their radars, which they were using, and presumably Flensburg as well. The most probable explanation is that it was a day fighter on a night cross-country that had forgotten to switch off its navigation lights, that just happened to be in the right place at the right time.

Flight sergeant McLean's ammunition mix had much to commend it, inasmuch as the 'fright factor' of so much tracer, combined with the penetrative power of armour-piercing bullets, was potentially very effective. But not all bomber crews thought this way; some preferred to fire no tracer at all on the grounds that this merely demonstrated the inadequate range of the .303 Brownings, thereby encouraging the night fighters to stand

off and shoot back. In fact, McLean's idea would only be effective if the fighter could be lured in close, which of course was done.

There can be no doubt that the corkscrew saved the lives of hundreds of bomber crewmen. However, to be really effective it had to be violent, as if it was too gently executed, an experienced fighter pilot could simply follow the bomber through the manoeuvre. Properly carried out, it made the bomber a very difficult target, even by day.

In the closing months of the war, Lancasters carried out many daylight raids over Germany. Whereas American heavy bombers flew in tightly packed formations to take advantage of the massed firepower of their heavy machine-guns, the reach of the Lancaster guns was less. The latter therefore flew in loose gaggles rather than tight formation, and corkscrewed when attacked by fighters. The combination of fire and movement generally proved an effective defence.

RAF LANCASTER SQUADRONS FORMED NOV 1942–DEC 1945

Squadron	First operation	Base formed
101	20/21 Nov 1942, Turin	Holme-on-Spalding Moor
103	21/22 Nov 1942, Gardening	Elsham Wolds
12	3/4 Jan 1943, Gardening	Wickenby
156	26/27 Jan 1943, Lorient	Warboys
100	4/5 Mar 1943, Gardening	Grimsby
115	20/21 Mar 1943, Gardening	East Wretham
617	16/17 May 1943, Dams Raid	Scampton
619	11/12 June 1943, Dusseldorf	Woodhall Spa
7	8/9 July 1943, Cologne	Oakington
514	3/4 Sep 1943, Dusseldorf	Foulsham
166	22/23 Sep 1943, Hanover	Kirmington
625	18/19 Oct 1943, Hanover	Kelstern
626	10/11 Nov 1943, Modane	Wickenby
550	26/27 Nov 1943, Berlin	Grimsby
576	2/3 Dec 1943, Berlin	Elsham Wolds
630	18/19 Dec 1943, Berlin	East Kirkby

RAF LANCASTER SQUADRONS FORMED JAN 1944–MAY 1945

Squadron	First operation	Base formed
622	14/15 Jan 1944, Brunswick	Mildenhall
15	Jan 1944, not known	Mildenhall
635	22/23 Mar 1944, Frankfurt	Downham Market
35	April 1944, not known	Graveley
582	9/10 April 1944, Lille	Little Staughton
90	June 1944, not known	Tuddenham
149	17 Sep 1944, Boulogne	Methwold
218	Sep 1944, not known	Methwold
153	7 Oct 1944, Emmerich	Kirmington
227	11 Oct 1944, Walcheren	Bardney
186	18 Oct 1944, Bonn	Tuddenham
170	19/20 Oct 1944, Stuttgart	Kelstern
195	26 Oct 1944, Leverkusen	Witchford
189	1 Nov 1944, Homburg	Bardney
150	2 Nov 1944, not known	Fiskerton
138	29 Mar 1945, Hallendorf	Tuddenham

As a weapon of war the Lancaster was a bludgeon rather than a rapier. But circumstances alter cases, and when precision weapons were devised for special targets, the Lancaster became a scalpel.

Ruhr industry was dependent on hydro-electric power and water, supplied by several huge dams. The destruction of the largest of these would have a devastating effect on German armaments output. But no ordinary bomb was capable of smashing these concrete monsters. In the Weybridge offices of Vickers, a quiet genius called Barnes Wallis applied himself to the problem.

The solution he came up with was a large mine, which had to be placed with absolute precision against the inner face of the dams by flying at exactly 220mph (354km/hr) and 60ft (18m), releasing the weapon to an accuracy of less than one-fifth of a second. This called for a special squadron, trained specifically for the task. To lead it, the very experienced and dynamic Wing Commander Guy Gibson was chosen, and his aircrews were hand-picked from the best that Bomber Command could offer. They were a mixed bag – predominantly British, but including 26 Canadians, 12 Australians, two New Zealanders and a single American. It is less widely known that the ground crews and support tradesmen were also hand-picked, which made for an exceptionally efficient unit. Thus was the birth of No. 617 Squadron at Scampton in March 1943.

The mine, codenamed Upkeep, was a large cylindrical weapon weighing 9,250lb (4,200kg), over two-thirds of which was high explosive. Aircraft were taken from squadrons in No. 5 Group, as it had been found that 'low mileage, one careful owner' machines had better serviceability rates than those fresh from the factory, and modified. The bomb bay doors were removed and special brackets fitted, together with an electric motor to get Upkeep rotating at 500 revolutions per minute before release. The bomb bay was faired to front and rear of the mine in order to reduce drag, and the mid-upper turret was removed.

Right: Provisioning Lancaster, with modified bomb bay for Upkeep, and dorsal turret removed.
Below: An inert Upkeep falls clear of the dropping aircraft during trials at Reculver.
Left: To mark the 34th anniversary of the raid on the dams, a Lancaster reflew the mission in 1977.

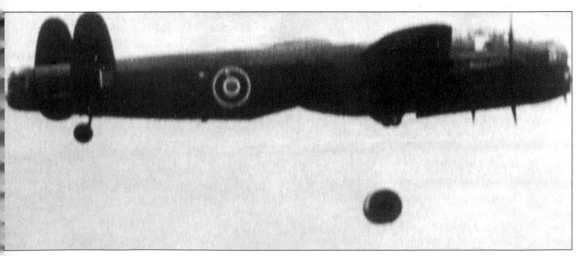

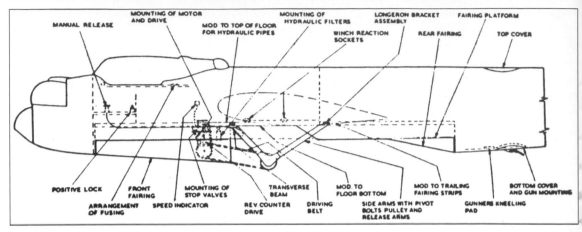

MANUAL RELEASE
MOUNTING OF MOTOR AND DRIVE
MOD TO TOP OF FLOOR FOR HYDRAULIC PIPES
MOUNTING OF HYDRAULIC FILTERS
WINCH REACTION SOCKETS
LONGERON BRACKET ASSEMBLY
REAR FAIRING
FAIRING PLATFORM
TOP COVER

POSITIVE LOCK
FRONT FAIRING
ARRANGEMENT OF FUSING
SPEED INDICATOR
MOUNTING OF STOP VALVES
REV. COUNTER DRIVE
TRANSVERSE BEAM
DRIVING BELT
MOD. TO FLOOR BOTTOM
SIDE ARMS WITH PIVOT BOLTS PULLEY AND RELEASE ARMS
MOD TO TRAILING FAIRING STRIPS
GUNNERS KNEELING PAD
BOTTOM COVER AND GUN MOUNTING

Above: Diagram of the modifications required to carry Upkeep. Surviving aircraft were converted back to original standard.

Transformed in this manner, Mk Is became Type 464 Provisioning Lancasters.

Other changes were made as they were found necessary. The entire raid was to be flown at low level, so bomb aimers assisted navigation using a specially prepared roller map. The nose turret had to be manned continually, which gave a role to the otherwise redundant mid-upper gunner, and stirrups were fitted to prevent him treading on the bomb-aimer's head in moments of excitement.

Achieving the exact height over water at night proved difficult, but was overcome by fitting Aldis lamps in the nose camera port and behind the bomb bay, angled so that the two spots of light touched at exactly 60ft (18m) and offset to starboard where they were easily seen by the navigator, who monitored height on the attack run.

This was the first use of the 'Master Bomber' technique, later to become standard

Standard bombsights could not be used, but the Dann sight, rigged up from a plywood triangle, an eyepiece and a couple of nails, worked well in

practice, while pilots had marks on the windshield to aid them in lining up on a target.

Close control of the operation was vital, and for this Gibson had all Lancasters fitted with fighter-type VHF radios. This was the first use of the 'Master Bomber' technique, later to become standard throughout Bomber Command.

At low level, the Lancasters might have to fight their way into and out of the target area, while the Mohne Dam at least was known to be defended. Three thousand rounds per gun was carried, giving 157 seconds of firing time. All of it was tracer, to keep the heads of the German gunners down.

■ OPERATION ■ CHASTISE

The attack on the dams was set for 16/17 May, when good weather was forecast, the moon was full, and the water level behind the dams was at its highest, Nineteen Lancasters took off in three waves. The first wave consisted of nine aircraft in three Vics of three, led by Gibson.

Left: Dr Barnes Wallis, creator of UpKeep, Tallboy and Grand Slam, pictured with the standard of No. 617 Squadron.
Below: Provisioning Lancaster at dispersal, showing the drive belt that rotated Upkeep at 500rpm before release.

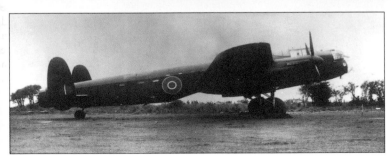

Above: Gibson leads his crew aboard Lancaster ED932, AJ-G, prior to taking off on the Dams Raid. His aircraft survived the war, only to be scrapped.

Left: ED825, AJ-T, was the reserve aircraft for the Dams Raid, and was flown by Flight Lieutenant McCarthy when his own machine went unserviceable.

Its primary targets were the Mohne and Eder Dams. The second wave, of five Lancasters flying individually, took a more northerly route. Their target was the Sorpe Dam, of different construction to the first two and needing a different mode of attack, albeit with the same weapon. The third and final wave of five aircraft also flew individually. Taking off two hours after the others, it was a reserve to be used against the main targets if needed, otherwise to attack secondary dams in the area.

Opposition to the passage of the first wave was moderate, but Bill Astell's Lancaster fell to light flak. The remainder arrived over the Mohne Dam on time. Gibson later wrote, "In that light it looked squat and heavy and unconquerable; it looked grey and solid in the moonlight, as though it were part of the countryside itself and just as immovable. A structure like a battleship was showering out flak all along its length."

After circling to make an assessment of the situation, Gibson began his attack run, curving in down-moon, past the hills and low over the water. He had his spotlights on for height, and the light flak saw him coming and opened up with everything they had, answered by Deering in the front turret. Bomb Aimer Spam Spafford released the mine, and they swept low over the dam. From the air it looked like a perfect drop, but in fact the mine had fallen short. The dam remained standing.

Next came Hopgood. He was not so lucky. Hit by flak, his aircraft was set on fire and crashed, while his mine bounced

Above: **Dams Raid debrief. Standing (left to right): Air Chief Marshal Arthur Harris, Air Marshal Cochrane. Seated: intelligence officer, Spafford and Taerum of Gibson's crew.**

Maudslay tried once more, but his mine hit the parapet with him just above it. For years it was assumed that he and his crew died in the explosion, but it appears that, badly damaged, he limped some 130 miles (210km) towards home before falling to flak.

Only one armed Lancaster remained, and on the second attempt its Australian pilot, Les Knight, made a perfect run. His mine punched a hole clean through the giant dam wall, and under the enormous pressure of water, the breach gradually widened.

The second wave of Lancasters had been less fortunate. The first aircraft to be lost during Operation Chastise was that of Byers, a Canadian, which was shot down by flak as it crossed the coast. In almost the same place, New Zealander Les Munro's Lancaster was damaged by flak and forced to abandon the mission, while Geoff Rice, flying as low as possible, hit the sea and lost his mine. Recovering by a hair's breadth, he also was forced to return. Barlow, an

clear over the dam. Gibson then made a critical move. Ordering Australian Mick Martin to attack, he flew slightly ahead of him and to one side to draw the enemy fire, and to add his own guns to Martin's in suppressing the defences. Even so, Martin's Lancaster was hit, and its mine was released off course to detonate harmlessly.

Fourth to attack was Dinghy Young, and with both Gibson and Martin distracting the defenders, he made a perfect run unscathed, and deposited his Upkeep right against the dam wall. Still the dam stood, but even as Maltby made his run, the parapet crumbled and the dam burst. His mine added to the breach made by Young.

■ ON TO THE EDER ■

Martin and Maltby now set course for home, while Gibson and Young, the latter acting as deputy leader, led the three remaining armed Lancasters to the Eder Dam.

This was undefended, for the Eder was surrounded by steep hills, making an attack very hazardous. Australian David Shannon made three attempts at it without being able to line up correctly. Henry Maudslay then tried twice, with no better luck. Shannon's fourth attempt run was accurate; his mine exploded against the dam, causing a small breach.

OPERATION CHASTISE, PARTICIPANTS

PILOT	LETTERS	AIRCRAFT NO.
First wave		
Wg Cdr G.P. Gibson	AJ-G	ED 932/G
Flt Lt J. V. Hopgood	AJ-M	ED 925/G
Flt Lt H.B. Martin	AJ-P	ED 909/G
Sqn Ldr H.M. Young	AJ-A	ED 887/G
Flt Lt D.J.H. Maltby	AJ-J	ED 906/G
Flt Lt D.J. Shannon	AJ-L	ED 929/G
Sqn Ldr H.M. Maudslay	AJ-Z	ED 937/G
Flt Lt W. Astell	AJ-B	ED 864/G
Plt Off L.G. Knight	AJ-N	ED 912/G
Second wave		
Flt Lt J.C. McCarthy	AJ-T	ED 825/G
Flt Lt R.N.G. Barlow	AJ-E	ED 927/G
Flt Lt J.L. Munro	AJ-W	ED 921/G
Plt Off V.W. Byers	AJ-K	ED 934/G
Plt Off G. Rice	AJ-H	ED 936/G
Third and reserve wave		
Plt Off W.H.T. Ottley	AJ-C	ED 910/G
Plt Off L.J. Burpee	AJ-S	ED 865/G
Flt Sgt K.S. Brown	AJ-F	ED 918/G
Flt Sgt W.C. Townsend	AJ-O	ED 886/G
Flt Sgt C.T. Anderson	AJ-Y	ED 914/G

Note: McCarthy was originally scheduled to fly ED 923/G, but this aircraft developed a hydraulic leak.

Australian, was claimed by flak just inside the German border, and of the ill-fated second wave, only the American Joe McCarthy survived. After making nine runs against the Sorpe, he dropped his mine on the tenth, but without any visible results.

The final wave fared only slightly better. Burpee, a young Canadian from Gibson's previous squadron, went down over Holland, while Ottley lasted only a little longer. Both fell to light flak. Of the other three, all Flight Sergeants, Anderson was the least lucky. Last off, the fates conspired to force him to abandon the mission without attacking.

One Victoria Cross and no fewer than 33 other awards were made

Brown attacked the Sorpe after several attempts, like McCarthy with no visible result, while Townsend, on couse for the Mohne Dam, was diverted to the Ennerpe Dam instead. After several brushed with flak, he emerged into an area made unrecognizable by floods from the already breached Mohne and Eder. Finally, Townsend arrived at what appeared to be the Ennerpe and dropped his mine, but post-war evidence seems to indicate that he attacked the Bever Dam 5 miles (8km) away.

Although the entire German air defence system was by now alert to the events, losses were lighter on the run home. Apart from Maudslay, the only other loss was Dinghy Young. Hit by flak as he recrossed the coast, he went down into the sea. Others, including McCarthy, Brown and Townsend, had eventful return flights, but recovered safely to Scampton.

Success had been dearly bought. Eight Lancasters failed to return home; of the 56 men on board them, only three survived. Gibson was awarded the Victoria Cross, Britain's highest decoration, and no fewer than 33 other awards were made to participants in the raid.

Above: The Dortmund-Ems Canal, scene of the Dam Busters' worst disaster, was finally breached in 1944. (Alfred Price)
Below: Under the leadership of Group Captain Leonard Cheshire VC, No. 617 Squadron became the most accurate heavy bomber squadron of the war.

The Dams Raid had long passed into legend. No. 617 Squadron had established itself as an elite unit; truly a special squadron. Over the next two years, it would fully maintain this reputation.

The Dams Raid over, a new role was sought for No. 617 Squadron. The modified Lancasters were replaced by standard Mk IIIs, and the crews started intensive high- and low-level training. Wing Commander Guy Gibson was replaced by Squadron Leader George Holden. A few unexciting trips to Italy followed; then, on 30 August 1943, the squadron was ordered to Coningsby to concentrate on low-level attacks.

■ DORTMUND-EMS ■

The next target was the heavily defended Dortmund-Ems canal, a strategic artery in the German transport system. Bomber Command had often attempted to breach its banks, but without success. Now 617 was to try, using the new 12,000lb (5,440kg) high-capacity bomb.

Low cloud in the target area caused the first attempt to be recalled, minus Maltby, who went into the sea after hitting someone's slipstream at low level. On the following night they tried again. It was a diaster. Heavy mist in the target area foiled all attempts to bomb

Above: No. 9 Squadron, pictured here with its famous W4964 *Johnny Walker*, was something of an elite outfit. Its total of 106 operations took in the Ruhr, Hamburg, Berlin and Peenemunde and *Tirpitz*.

accurately, while the defences claimed five Lancasters, among them those of Holden and Les Knight. The squadron rapidly gained the reputation of being a suicide outfit. This notwithstanding, six aircraft, in company with six more from No. 619 Squadron, went out again the following night to attack the Antheor Viaduct in southern France at low level. This was another failure, and the squadron was withdrawn from operations while changes took place.

One was the introduction of the extremely accurate Stabilizing Automatic Bomb Sight, or SABS, introduced by

Arthur 'Talking Bomb' Richardson, whom we last saw over Gdynia with Guy Gibson. No. 617 was now to become a medium- and high-level 'sniper' squadron. The other was the arrival of Wing Commander Leonard Cheshire to command on 11 November.

A more exacting test came on the night of 8/9 February

Cheshire was an enigma. Introspective and unconventional, he was arguably the most inspirational bomber leader of the war. Always leading from the front, he has been described by David

Shannon as a pied piper; people followed him gladly. He now set out to make the squadron live, breathe and eat bombing accuracy.

Several missions followed against pinpoint targets, but they were not a great success. Oboe marking was too inaccurate against small targets. Cheshire and Martin worked out between them that only low-level marking in a dive would be good enough, and on 3/4 January 1944 they tried it against a flying bomb site at Freval. By the illumination of flares they marked from 400ft (120m), and 12,000lb (5,440kg) bombs from the remainder of the formation obliterated the target.

A more exacting test came on 8/9 February, by which time No. 617 had moved to Woodhall Spa. The aero engine works at Limoges were almost totally destroyed after being marked at low level, while damage to French houses close by was minimal. Other raids followed with equal success, the only failure during this time being another attempt against the Antheor Viaduct.

To mark heavily defended targets, a smaller and faster aircraft was needed. The obvious choice was a Mosquito, which Cheshire duly acquired, bringing the low-level marking career of the Lancaster to an end. At the same time, 617 became pathfinders and Main Force leaders to No. 5 Group. But other plans for them were afoot.

■ D-DAY DECEPTION ■

The first of these was Operation Taxable, a deception ploy that was designed to make the Germans think that a vast invasion fleet was moving towards Cap d'Antifer, some 20 miles (30km) north of Le Havre. This was done by 16 Lancasters, flying precise speeds and courses, dropping Window at five-second intervals. Packed to the gills with Window bundles, they maintained the deception for some eight hours, until dawn broke to reveal only an empty sea to the expectant Germans.

The second was the introduction of the Tallboy, a new 12,000lb (5,440kg) bomb with exceptionally good ballistic qualities and penetrative power. Like Upkeep, Tallboy was the brainchild of Dr Barnes Wallis, and only the SABS-equipped Dam Busters could bomb accurately enough to make the best use of this new and devastating weapon.

Above: Lurking in the Norwegian fjords, the German battleship *Tirpitz* kept strong British naval forces tied down.

MOHNE DAM

"The gunners had seen us coming. They could see us coming with our spotlights on for over two miles away. Now they opened up and tracers began swirling towards us; some were even bouncing on the smooth surface of the lake. This was a horrible moment: we were being dragged along at four miles a minute, almost against our will, towards the things we were going to destroy. I think at that moment the boys did not want to go. I know I did not wat to go."

WING COMMANDER G. PENROSE GIBSON
VC, DSO, DFC

One of the few south-to-north rail routes still open in France at this time passed through a tunnel near Saumur, on the Loire. Shortly after midnight on 8/9 June the squadron arrived overhead, and Cheshire placed two red spot fires in the mouth of the tunnel. Nineteen Tallboy-armed Lancasters moved in, plus another six with more conventional loads. The result was a series of enormous craters that tore the line to pieces. One Tallboy, however, had impacted the hillside and bored its way down to explode actually inside the tunnel almost 60ft (18m) below, completely blocking it.

Other precision raids followed: concrete E-boat pens at Le Havre, and V- Weapon sites scattered around the Pas-de-Calais and elsewhere. Then, in

July, command of the squadron passed from Cheshire to Wing Commander Willie Tait DSO DFC.

■ 617 VERSUS *TIRPITZ* ■

The German battleship *Tirpitz* had long been a thorn in the side of the Royal Navy. Lying in Alten Fjord in northern Norway, by its very existence it tied down British naval units which would have been better employed elsewhere.

Even from the most northerly of British airfields, Alten Fjord was outside Lancaster range. A deal was struck with the Russians, who made Yagodnik, near

EVADING RADAR

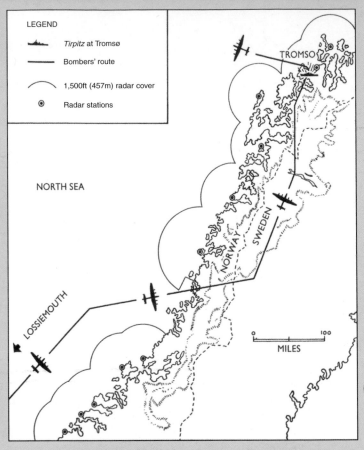

LEGEND

⬚ *Tirpitz* at Tromsø

─── Bombers' route

⌒ 1,500ft (457m) radar cover

◉ Radar stations

TROMSO

NORTH SEA

NORWAY

SWEDEN

LOSSIEMOUTH

0　100
MILES

Evading the German radar cover by flying in over Sweden, Nos. 617 and 9 Squadrons achieved complete surprise in their third attack on the *Tirpitz*.

system proved equal to the task, and a smokescreen quickly obscured the battleship. This notwithstanding, a single Tallboy hit was scored, but *Tirpitz* was still afloat. The Kriegsmarine moved her south to Tromsø for use as a floating gun battery; she would never sail again, but this was not known either.

Calculations showed that fitting internal fuel tanks in the fuselage of the Lancasters would just allow the monster to be attacked from Lossiemouth. On 20 October, 40 aircraft of 617 and 9 Squadrons set out on the long haul to Tromsø. A combination of poor weather and enemy fighters made this attack a failure, and few crews even so much as saw the battleship.

They achieved complete surprise and scored multiple hits

The final attack on *Tirpitz* was mounted on 12 November, with 31 Lancasters from both squadrons. Approaching from the neutral (Swedish) side, they achieved complete surprise and scored multiple hits. The *Tirpitz* slowly turned turtle, but the water was too shallow for her to sink completely.

Below: "Twas a famous victory!" *Tirpitz* lies belly up in Tromsø Fjord, having capsized after multiple bomb hits.

Arkhangelsk, available as a refuelling stop. For this and subsequent anti-*Tirpitz* operations, No. 617 was joined by No. 9 Squadron, which, although fitted with the Mk XIV vector bombsight, was also something of an elite outfit. Of the 36 Lancasters detailed, 24 carried Tallboys; the others were loaded with 12 Johnny Walker Diving Mines each, an original but ineffective weapon.

The raid nearly ended in disaster as bad weather over Russia forced many Lancasters to land where they could. Six were abandoned in the marshes. When on 15 September the attack was finally mounted, the German early warning

Above: Lancasters of No. 101 Squadron were identifiable by their Air-borne Cigar masts. This one is unloading incendiaries.

Tait was now replaced by 617's final wartime commander, Group Captain John Fauquier, a Canadian. Tallboys now rained down on the U-boat pens at Bergen, and the Bielefeld Viaduct. In common with most bridges, the latter proved singularly hard to hit, and 54 Tallboys were aimed at it during February 1945 without result. But now Barnes Wallis' 22,000lb (10 tonne) Grand Slam was ready for use.

Only the Lancaster B.I Special could carry Grand Slam. This aircraft had strengthened main gear, nose and dorsal turrets deleted, and the bomb doors removed, plus other minor modifications. The crew was reduced to four.

The first Grand Slam raid took place on 14 March 1945, as related earlier. Five days later, six Grand Slams and 13 Tallboys were hauled to the rail viaduct at Arnsberg, where, incredibly, every bomb fell within a 600ft (180m) radius. To underline the astounding level of bombing accuracy, when the bridge at Nienberg was attacked on 22 March, the first four aircraft sent in to bomb scored direct hits from a Grand Slam at one end and a Tallboy at the other, and lifted the entire centre span into the air, where it was hit straight in the middle by another Tallboy!

The final mission was against Berchtesgaden Hitler's redoubt

One more bridge was smashed, then the U-boat pens at Farge were attacked. Two Grand Slams went clean through the 23ft (7m) thick reinforced concrete roof and exploded inside, while shock waves from 10 near misses shattered the foundation. 617 Squadron's final mission was against Berchtesgaden, Hitler's southern redoubt, in the final days of the war.

There was one other special Lancaster squadron, No. 101, whose aircraft, aerials, carried the top secret ABC (Air-borne Cigar) from October 1943. ABC was a jammer working on the German night fighter frequency, and required an additional member of crew to operate it. Lancasters of No. 101 Squadron carried a full load of bombs and, scattered throughout the bomber stream, accompanied Main Force on nearly every raid. In the later stages of the war, with multi-pronged raids the norm, 101 became the biggest Lancaster squadron of all, with a final complement of 42 aircraft.

Although built in large numbers and with many variants, the Lancaster's external appearance changed little during its production, and its overall dimensions not at all.

LANCASTER MK I

Basic data for the Lancaster given in tabular form in Chapter 2 applies to the Mk I Merlin XX or XXII engines. Production continued past the end of the war, and the final Lancaster ever built was a Mk I. Many were later fitted with H2S, and others had bulged bomb bay doors to allow them to carry 8,000 and 12,000lb (3,600 and 5,440kg) HC bombs.

Lancaster Mk I raided Nuremberg and Dresden while with No. 170 Squadron. It is seen here post-war, testing tyres for Dunlop.

LANCASTER MK I VARIANTS

Provisioning Lancasters used on the Dams Raid were converted Mk Is. Mk I Special was designed to carry 22,000lb (10 tonne) Grand Slam with a maximum overload weight of 70,000lb (31,750kg). No nose or mid-upper turret. Only 32 built. Mk I (FE) intended for the Far East against Japan, but the war ended before they could arrive. Internal fuel capacity was increased to 2,554 gal (11,600 litres); range with 7,000lb (3,175kg) bomb load 3,180 miles (5,100km); FN 82 rear turrets were standard.

A saddle tank was designed to increase fuel capacity for Far East operations, but in high temperatures, take-off became marginal. (Alfred Price)

LANCASTER MK II

Powered by four Bristol Hercules VI or XVI 14-cylinder radial engines each rated at 1,735hp. Rate of climb was about 5 per cent less than that of the Mks I and III; service ceiling was lower at 22,000ft (6,700m); maximum and cruising speeds were rather lower, mainly due to the extra drag of the radial engines. Range with 12,000lb (5,440kg) was 1,000 miles (1,600km). Maximum overload weight was 63,000lb (28,600kg). A few Mk IIs were fitted with a single .50 calibre machine-gun in the ventral position.

LANCASTER MK III

Virtually identical to the Mk I, the main difference being Packard-built Rolls-Royce Merlin 28s or 38s. These were popular with the engine fitters because of the lavish tool kits provided by the Americans. As with the Mk I, bulged bomb bay doors and H2S were often fitted. Many late-build aircraft carried the Rose Rice tail turret.

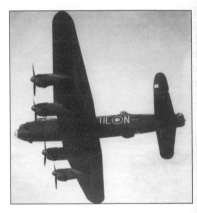

The Lancaster Mk III was virtually identical to the Mk I.

Lancaster IIs of No. 408 'Goose' Squadron RCAF based at Linton-on-Ouse in October 1943.

The Lancaster Mk IV and V were so different from the original that they were renamed Lincoln B.1 and B.2.

LANCASTER MK IV AND V

Essentially a stretched Lancaster, longer, with greater wingspan, and better performance, the Mks IV and V differed so much that they were renamed Lincoln I and II.

The engine cowlings to the Merlin 85/87s on the Mk VI differed appreciably from those of earlier models.

LANCASTER MK VI

Nine aircraft only, converted from Mk Is and IIIs, used in the Pathfinder and ECM roles by No. 635 Squadron. Powered by Merlin 85s or 87s rated at 1,635hp enclosed in redesigned cowling, driving four-bladed propellers. Performance was significantly better than that of the Mk III. No production undertaken.

LANCASTER MK VII

Final production variant. Martin mid-upper and Rose Rice tail turrets. Entered service April 1945. A few Mk VII (FE)s were built.

The final production variant was the Mk VII, with .50in guns in mid-upper and tail turrets. This is a Mk VII (FE) intended for Tiger Force.

LANCASTER MK X

Canadian-built Mk III.

The Mk X was a Canadian-built Mk III. This machine, seen at the Malton works still minus its mid-upper turret, served with No. 428 'Ghost' Squadron RCAF.

POST-WAR LANCASTER CONVERSIONS

ASR III, Mk III converted for air-sea rescue with an airborne lifeboat fitted to the bomb bay, and ASV radar. Dorsal turret was removed, and guns removed from rear turret. Small windows to both sides of rear fuselage. Re-engined with Merlin 224s

Conversion to ASR III standard, with paradroppable airborne lifeboat. Most later converted to MR/GR III.

GR III/MR III, Mk III converted for general reconnaissance or maritime reconnaissance similar to ASR III, but no lifeboat.

Experimental ASV radar aerial mounting, intended for use in the anti-shipping role. (Alfred Price)

PR I, Mk I converted for photo reconnaissance/survey work. All gun turrets were removed and faired over.

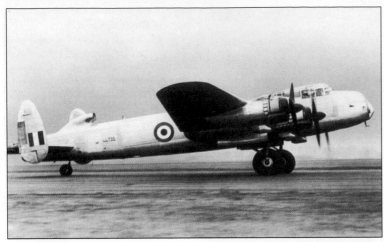

many of her Lancasters home, while the French Aeronavale acquired a considerable number for maritime reconnaissance and search and rescue, a few of which remained in service up until the early 1960s. Other users were Argentina and Egypt.

In Britain, the writing was on the wall. The Lincoln largely replaced the Lancaster in the few remaining front-line bomber squadrons, and the last RAF Lancaster, an MR III, was retired in February 1954.

Into the jet age. This Mk II spent its life at the RAE Farnborough as a test bed for early jet engines.

The end of the war saw dozens of Bomber Command Lancaster Squadrons disbanded and hundreds of aircraft scrapped, but this did not prevent another 21 squadrons from other RAF commands operating the type. Other countries used them too – Canada took

Jet Age II – a Canadian Mk X-DC drone carrier, with Ryan Firebees beneath the wingtips.

This propeller from a shot-down Lancaster of No. 12 Squadron makes a fitting memorial at Dronten in Holland.

BIBLIOGRAPHY

Books

Avro Lancaster by Francis K. Mason, Aston Publications, 1989.

Battle Over the Reich by Alfred Price, Ian Allan, 1973.

British Aircraft Armament, Vols. 1 and 2 by R. Wallace Clarke, Patrick Stephens Ltd, 1993/94.

Dam Busters by Paul Brickhill, Pan, 1954.

Enemy Coast Ahead by Guy Gibson VC, Pan, 1955.

Famous Bombers of the Second World War by William Green, MacDonald & Janes, 1975.

Instruments of Darkness by Alfred Price, MacDonald & Janes, 1977.

Nuremberg Raid by Martin Middlebrook, Fontana, 1975.

Pathfinder by D.C.T. Bennett, Frederick Muller, 1958.

617 Squadron, The Dam Busters at War by Tom Bennett, Patrick Stephens Ltd, 1985.

Magazines

Various issues of *Air International, Flypast* and *RAF Flying Review*.

ABOUT THE AUTHOR

Mike Spick is a full-time writer and commentator in the aviation scene. His specialities are fighter tactics and helicopter warfare, and he spent several years as a consultant to the Swiss-based Project Atlas. He is an Associate of the Royal Aeronautical Society and has written over 40 books on military aviation, including *Luftwaffe Bomber Aces, Allied Fighter Aces* and *Luftwaffe Fighter Aces*. He has also contributed to many publications, including *Air International, Air Enthusiast* and *Asia Pacific Defence Reporter*. He has advised on aviation matters for television, and is a consultant to the magazine *Air Forces Monthly*.